At Issue

Voter Fraud

Other Books in the At Issue Series:

At Issue

Voter Fraud

Roman Espejo, Book Editor

GREENHAVEN PRESS
A part of Gale, Cengage Learning

Detroit • New York • San Francisco • New Haven, Conn • Waterville, Maine • London

Christine Nasso, *Publisher*
Elizabeth Des Chenes, *Managing Editor*

© 2010 Greenhaven Press, a part of Gale, Cengage Learning.

Gale and Greenhaven Press are registered trademarks used herein under license.

For more information, contact:
Greenhaven Press
27500 Drake Rd.
Farmington Hills, MI 48331-3535
Or you can visit our Internet site at gale.cengage.com

For product information and technology assistance, contact us at

Gale Customer Support, 1-800-877-4253

For permission to use material from this text or product, submit all requests online at
www.cengage.com/permissions

Further permissions questions can be emailed to permissionrequest@cengage.com

Articles in Greenhaven Press anthologies are often edited for length to meet page requirements. In addition, original titles of these works are changed to clearly present the main thesis and to explicitly indicate the author's opinion. Every effort is made to ensure that Greenhaven Press accurately reflects the original intent of the authors. Every effort has been made to trace the owners of copyrighted material.

Cover photograph © Images.com/Corbis.

LIBRARY OF CONGRESS CATALOGING-IN-PUBLICATION DATA

Voter fraud / Roman Espejo, book editor.
    p. cm. -- (At issue)
    Includes bibliographical references and index.
    ISBN 978-0-7377-4693-8 (hardcover) -- ISBN 978-0-7377-4694-5 (pbk.)
    1. Elections--Corrupt practices--United States. 2. Political corruption--United
States. I. Espejo, Roman, 1977-
    JK1994.V68 2010
    324.6'60973--dc22
                                                    2009047747

Printed in the United States of America
1 2 3 4 5 6 7 14 13 12 11 10

Contents

Introduction

ACORN (Association of Community Organizations for Reform Now) came under fire during the 2008 presidential election. In October of that year, the community-action organization announced that its 8,000 hired canvassers had registered 1.3 million new voters in twenty-one states. However, after the registration forms were reviewed by ACORN auditors, 400,000 were tossed out because they were duplicates, incomplete, or bogus—filled out with fictitious names like Mickey Mouse. Thousands more were from registered individuals who had made changes of address. As a result, the tally of first-time voters that ACORN canvassers signed up was recalculated to 450,000.

In a 2008 *New York Times* article, reporters Michael Falcone and Michael Moss stated, "In registration drives, it is common for a percentage of newly registered voters to be disqualified for various reasons, although experts say the percentage is higher when groups pay workers to gather registrations."[1] Critics, particularly conservatives, cried foul and charged ACORN with engaging in deliberate fraud to skew the elections in favor of liberals. "The group is really tainted, and any work they do is suspect," argued Danny Diaz, spokesman of the Republican National Committee.[2] Political commentator Michelle Malkin claimed, "The group's vandalism on electoral integrity is systemic."[3] She cited purported instances of ACORN voter fraud dating back to 2004, including the registration of underage and deceased individuals. And an ACORN worker in Pennsylvania was found guilty of falsifying twenty-nine registration forms in March 2008.

1. Oct. 23, 2008.
2. *New York Times*, Oct. 23, 2008.
3. http://townhall.com, June 25, 2008.

ACORN defended its voter registration efforts, which are intended to increase turnout among groups in which participation in elections is historically low. Brian Kettenring, an ACORN spokesman, maintained, "Everybody knows that when 1.3 million applications are submitted, not every single one of them gets on the rolls."[4] Furthermore, supporters uphold that to its credit, ACORN had flagged and reported the invalid forms itself and committed no wrongdoing. According to blogger Shelley Powers, "ACORN, any voter registration organization, cannot discard any voter registration card. By law. This is so that organizations can't 'pretend' to register folks, and then discard the registrations in an attempt to rig the vote."[5]

The ACORN controversy was the crux of the voter-fraud debate during the decade's groundbreaking presidential race. Albeit unrelated to elections or voters, a sting-operation scandal hit ACORN in September 2009, resulting in the end of its promotional partnership with the U.S. Census Bureau and the U.S. House of Representatives' vote to discontinue federal funding of the organization. One analysis reports that ACORN has received $53 million directly from the government since 1994.

ACORN may have suffered a critical setback, but voter fraud remains a point of contention along party lines. Many Republicans allege that it is widespread. For instance, the *Washington Post* reported that almost half of the dozen attorneys removed or considered for dismissal at the U.S. Department of Justice in 2006 were accused by conservatives of failing to sufficiently confront the issue. Staff writers Dan Eggen and Amy Goldstein wrote, "The behind-the-scenes maneuvering to replace U.S. attorneys viewed as weak on voter fraud,

4. *New York Times*, Oct. 23, 2008.
5. http://shelleypowers.burningbird.net, Oct. 14, 2008.

from state Republican parties to the White House, is one element of a nationwide partisan brawl over voting rights in recent years."[6] Former Attorney General Alberto R. Gonzales described the prosecution of illegal election activities as "an obligation."[7]

Democrats, on the other hand, perceive voter disenfranchisement and a lack of representation among low-income households, minorities, and the elderly as the real problem. In fact, in the House's decision to strip ACORN of taxpayer support, all of the opposing seventy-five votes were submitted by liberals. Regarding voter fraud, Missouri Secretary of State Robin Carnahan contends, "Like the myth of Bigfoot, the more folks hear about it, the more they might think it is true." She continues that "this can hinder voter confidence and discourage participation."[8]

The issue of voter fraud is not limited to improper registration forms or voter oppression. Electronic voting machines, electoral districts, human error, stricter identification requirements, and voting by mail also emerge as issues at the forefront of the debate. The authors in *At Issue: Voter Fraud* present contrasting perspectives on these concerns and examine the status of the vote in America.

6. May 14, 2007.
7. *Washington Post*, May 14, 2007.
8. www.alternet.org, Mar. 14, 2008.

1

Voter Fraud Is a Myth

Daphne Eviatar

Daphne Eviatar is a lawyer and journalist based in Brooklyn, N.Y. She also is a senior reporter for the American Lawyer.

Evidence shows that voter fraud is extremely rare; harassment and intimidation at the polls are the real issues. Close elections, as seen during the 2000 presidential race, also are unlikely. Nonetheless, the Republican Party uses the myth to justify unfair restrictions on voting and influence the outcomes of elections. Unwarranted obstructions include matching registration data with state databases, heightened identification requirements, and other procedures that disenfranchise thousands of eligible voters—mainly minorities, the poor, and the elderly. And although most have failed, the spate of legal attacks and investigations by conservatives threaten to undermine legitimate elections and discourage new groups of voters.

Earlier this month [in October 2008], Republicans in Ohio lost their lawsuit challenging a state rule that allows voters to register and vote early on the same day. But the state party had no intention of conceding the point. GOP [Grand Old Party, or Republican] officials demanded records from all 88 county boards of election identifying every person who took advantage of same-day registration and voting. In one county, the Republican district attorney even opened a grand jury investigation.

"He's investigating people who the law says are allowed to vote," said Ohio ACLU [American Civil Liberties Union] law-

Daphne Eviatar, "A Myth of Voter Fraud," *Washington Independent*, October 28, 2008. Reproduced by permission.

yer Carrie Davis. After it was revealed that the district attorney was also the local chairman of the [Republican candidate John] McCain campaign, he was forced to appoint a special prosecutor to handle the case.

There's no indication that any of these voters did anything illegal. But the attempt to investigate voters who took advantage of a state rule designed to encourage voter participation exemplifies the kinds of attacks on new voters that are going on across the country.

Even when the challenges fail, Republican officials persist in their claims of voter fraud in what appears to be an effort to lay the groundwork for challenging the outcome of Election Day. In about a dozen interviews, legal scholars and voting experts say this broad-based attack could lead to serious and continuing challenges to the legitimacy of the next president.

"[Republicans are] trying to do what they can to poison the well on the eve of the election because they're not winning on the issues," contends Charles Lichtman, statewide lead counsel for the Florida Democratic Party. The party, like the Obama campaign, is assembling a team of volunteer lawyers to take on unwarranted challenges and obstruction to voters on Election Day. "They know there are more Democrats registered than Republicans," said Lichtman, "so they're calling out fraud where it didn't occur."

For months now, Republicans have been claiming that voter fraud is rampant and that government officials aren't sufficiently cracking down. Democrats insist that voter fraud is practically nonexistent—the real problem is intimidation and harassment of voters at the polls, they say.

Voting-rights experts tend to agree with the Democrats. A study by the Brennan Center for Justice, for example, found that, "It's more likely that an individual will be struck by lightning than that he will impersonate another voter at the polls."

Another study, by Barnard College political scientist Lori Minnite, similarly concluded that voter fraud is "extremely rare." The Brennan Center also showed that the sort of strict rules advocated by Republicans in Wisconsin, Ohio and elsewhere would disenfranchise thousands of people—usually the poor, elderly and minorities.

Even official Justice Dept. policy had acknowledged until recently that individual voter fraud has "only a minimal impact on the integrity of the voting process."

Even the most rigorous studies, however, haven't made the issue any less of a political football. Republicans like Cleta Mitchell, an election lawyer who chairs the Republican National Lawyers Assn., says such experts are just part of "the professional vote-fraud deniers industry," insisting that voting fraud exists even if it's nearly impossible to prove.

"If you just deny it," Mitchell said, "then that means that anyone who wants to take any steps to protect the integrity of the process can only be doing that because they're a racist."

In fact, even official Justice Dept. policy had acknowledged until recently that individual voter fraud has "only a minimal impact on the integrity of the voting process" and therefore usually wasn't worth trying to prosecute. Then last year, the [George W.] Bush administration changed that to allow individual prosecutors to pursue such cases at their discretion.

When some U.S. attorneys refused because of a lack of evidence, several were fired, contributing to the scandal that ultimately forced the resignation of Atty. Gen. Alberto Gonzales. Since then, Democrats have become even more vigilant in fighting back against claims of voter fraud.

"No Match, No Vote"

In many states—including Florida, Ohio, Wisconsin and Oregon—Republican officials have insisted that states square new voters' registration information with that in other state databases, such as motor vehicle or Social Security. While such matching is required by the Help America Vote Act of 2002, Republicans in swing states are insisting that the match be exact as a condition to vote.

Some of these "no-match, no-vote" states allow voters whose registration doesn't match to fill out a provisional ballot, but they must provide matching verification information to election officials within 48 hours or their votes won't count. In close swing states, which votes are counted could make all the difference to the outcome.

In Ohio, for example, Republicans sued Secretary of State Jennifer Brunner to make matching a condition of voting. In response, she argued that adopting such a rule could get some 200,000 Ohio voters kicked off the rolls. The problem is not that they're ineligible, for the most part. It's that the information doesn't match because voters have changed their names or because state workers have made clerical errors.

Earlier this month [October 2008], the U.S. Supreme Court sided with Brunner. Ruling on procedural grounds, it found that the state GOP likely didn't have the right under federal law to challenge the Ohio law's application. So Ohio Republicans are taking their fight elsewhere. Last week, they sent a letter to U.S. Atty. Gen. Michael Mukasey asking him to force Ohio to require matching under federal law.

And on Friday, President George W. Bush himself got involved, asking Mukasey to investigate the status of the 200,000 non-matching Ohio voters.

The Republican attorney general in Wisconsin brought a similar challenge against his state's elections board, but it failed last week. (The attorney general plans to appeal the decision.) A Dane County judge ruled that, "Nothing in state or federal law requires that there be a data match as a condition on the right to vote." A matching requirement, the elections board had found, could have disenfranchised more than 20 percent of Wisconsin's registered voters.

Republicans have lost most of their legal challenges claiming states aren't adequately protecting against voter fraud. But legal experts worry that the steady barrage of legal attacks in battleground states is part of a broader effort to lay the groundwork for undermining the legitimacy of the outcome of the presidential election. That could further fuel the anger of the Republican base against the Democratic candidate—and possibly the next president.

"If it's close, and if, in the grand scheme of things, Ohio would make a difference in the Electoral College or the finally tally, all these aspersions could come into play in challenging those results," said Davis, the Ohio ACLU attorney. Either party could bring a legal challenge questioning the validity of provisional or absentee ballots.

While experts say it's rare to see the sort of scenario that occurred in Florida in 2000, where the outcome of the presidential election hinged on a few hundred votes in one state, the increased focus on voter problems and recent changes in voting laws means litigation over the outcome remains a real possibility.

"Besides Florida, you'd have to go back to the 19th century in the United States to get to an election that was that close," said Daniel Tokaji, a law professor at Ohio State University and an expert in election law. "Then again, in 2004 we weren't that far away—there were about 100,000 votes in Ohio on which the outcome depended. If we'd had a second litigated election in 2004, it would have been like lightning striking twice. So it could happen again."

Because of the close elections and revelations of voting problems in 2000 and 2004, said Tokaji, "we've got people paying much closer attention to the mechanics of elections." Also, "there are a lot of changes in the law. That always leads to more litigation, because there are issues of how those laws should be interpreted and applied."

Even if the election weren't close enough to merit legal challenges, many Democrats worry that the GOP claims of voter fraud are a preemptive attempt to undermine the legitimacy of a Barack Obama presidency.

"It's a desperate attempt to unfairly flavor and throw something out there and take people away from the real issues," said Lichtman of the Florida Democratic Party. Florida's voter registration rules, which require all voter registration information to match the state databases, have been the subject of ongoing litigation.

The History of Voter Fraud

Claims of voter fraud before an election are nothing new, of course. For centuries, strict-voter registration rules have been applied to limit access to voting, often targeting the poor and minority citizens.

"We've seen it throughout American history," said Tokaji. "In the 19th century, claims of fraud were made to exclude immigrants, ethnic minorities and laborers. And throughout most of the 20th century, the disenfranchisement of African-Americans in the South was done through voter-registration requirements that local officials claimed were to prevent voter fraud."

More recently, Republicans have been claiming widespread voter fraud to tighten requirements on who can vote. "They're trying to use the so-called epidemic of voter fraud to justify voter ID laws," said Gerald Hebert, a senior elections official at the Justice Dept. from 1973–1994 and who is executive director of the Campaign Legal Center, a nonpartisan organization focusing on election reform.

That's how Indiana came to pass its voter-identification law. When that law was challenged, the Supreme Court acknowledged there was no evidence of voter fraud in Indiana.

Still, the court upheld, by a vote of 6 to 3, the state's requirement that voters present a state-issued photo identification card before casting a ballot, finding that it did not impose an unjustified burden on the poor, minorities or others less likely to have such a photo ID

Associate law professor Michael Pitts at Indiana University studied the effects of the new law. He found the votes of 80 percent of Indiana residents forced to fill out a provisional ballot because they didn't have the required I.D. card were never counted.

The ACORN Controversy

Recent revelations that some workers from the Assn. of Community Organizations for Reform Now, or ACORN, have turned in fraudulent registration forms has fanned the flames of this dispute, leading to calls for more voter-identification laws, as well as no-match, no-vote requirements.

The overwhelming evidence is that fraudulent voter registrations do not lead to fraudulent voting.

But Republicans' claims against ACORN have gone further. Legislators and party officials have used the false registrations to claim that ACORN is engaging in an effort to steal the election for the Democratic Party. Investigations of fraudulent activity are going on in at least 10 states, and the Justice Dept. has reportedly begun an investigation of ACORN, a community-organizing group that advocates on behalf of low-income families, following requests from numerous Republicans.

Sen. John Cornyn (R-Tex.), for example, a member of the Senate Judiciary Committee, wrote to Mukasey earlier this month, urging him to investigate ACORN as a "criminal enterprise."

The Obama campaign and former Dept. of Justice lawyers involved in voting-rights issues say such an investigation before the election might intimidate legitimate voters and violate Justice Dept. policy.

ACORN has repeatedly explained that when its workers submitted false registrations, the fraud was against ACORN, not against voters or the elections process. That's because the duplicate or made-up registration forms were mostly turned in by workers who ACORN paid to sign up voters in their neighborhoods.

That some of those workers copied names out of the phone book, or listed their favorite cartoon characters, doesn't mean those people are going to show up to vote. But it does mean that ACORN didn't get it's money's worth. The group checks all submitted registration forms and flags for local election officials those that are suspect. In most states, it's still required by law to turn all forms in.

"The overwhelming evidence is that fraudulent voter registrations do not lead to fraudulent voting," said Wendy Weiser, a deputy director specializing in voting rights at New York University's Brennan Center for Justice. "It's a big resource drain on election officials, but it doesn't affect the outcome."

That hasn't stopped the allegations. Sen. John McCain's claim in the last debate that ACORN is potentially committing "one of the greatest frauds of voter history in this country, maybe destroying the fabric of democracy" has helped set the stage for broad claims of a stolen election after Nov. 4.

McCain's remarks were followed by violence. Within days, two ACORN offices were vandalized, and one organizer received a death threat. People for the American Way reports that ACORN offices have received a barrage of racist and threatening voicemails and emails.

ACORN's own exaggerations about its effectiveness in registering voters haven't helped. Last Thursday [October 23], the group admitted it had vastly overstated the number of legitimate new voters it registered this year, acknowledging that about 30 percent of the 1.3 million new voters it had claimed credit for were either duplicates or not real.

Though some percentage of erroneous applications is expected, both the large number of registered voters and the colorful news stories—about how characters like Mickey Mouse have registered, for example—encouraged Republicans to keep hammering away at charges that the liberal-leaning group, which advocates on behalf of low-income Americans expected to favor Sen. Barack Obama, is planning to steal the presidential election for Democrats.

Given the latest polls, it probably wouldn't need to. But election lawyers worry that the problems of voter registration by groups like ACORN provide an easy way for Republicans to later claim, if Obama wins, that he's not the legitimate president.

"It does seem like there is an attempt to cast the specter of voter fraud over this election," said Hebert. "Like there's an attempt to get people all riled up in the base of the Republican Party, to say, 'We're not going to let people steal our election.'"

2

Redistricting Is Not a Problem

FairVote

Founded in 1992 as the Center for Voting and Democracy, Fair-Vote is a nonprofit advocacy group in Takoma Park, Maryland.

Contrary to Democrat claims, the lack of competition in elections, as well as recent Republican advantages, cannot be attributed to campaign spending or gerrymandering, the forming of districts along party lines. Numerous races, for example, demonstrate that the amounts of money spent by candidates are not correlated with outcomes. Moreover, gerrymandering is not the root cause of noncompetition—elections were sharply tilted decades before regular redistricting and most incumbents did not need or gain from such mapping. Rather, political affairs and trends have set voting patterns, and leveling partisanship within districts will not increase competitiveness. Such efforts would have mixed impacts on representations of party, race, and gender.

After four decades of control of the U.S. House of Representatives, usually by overwhelming margins, some Democrats may have developed a sense of entitlement about running the House. When Republicans took control in the 1994 elections, it was not hard for these Democrats to point their fingers at culprits other than themselves for their defeats, including alleged Republican advantages won in redistricting and strategic campaign spending or untrustworthy voting machines. These perceptions were fueled by reformers eager to seize on an opportunity to make their case for reform. Some

"The Gerrymander and Money Myths," FairVote, 2006. Reproduced by permission.

showcased data that suggested money determines the outcomes in more than 90% of House races, while others focused on how new techniques for partisan gerrymandering were the biggest contributing factor to declines in electoral competition and increases in the general Republican advantage.

There is an element of truth to these claims. Certainly our antiquated mechanics of running elections result in literally millions of lost votes in national elections, congressional candidates would rather have more money to spend than less, and partisans would not wage such bitter political and legal fights over redistricting if they did not recognize its power to affect electoral outcomes. But FairVote challenges the underlying argument that either campaign spending or gerrymandering is the major reason for either the remarkable levels of non-competition in U.S. House races or for recent Republican advantages.

It's Not the Money: Our Intensive Examination of the 2000 Election Cycle

Because winning House races is strongly correlated with campaign spending and outspending one's opponent, in particular, some observers are quick to mistake cause for effect when it comes to money's place in U.S. House elections. Money flows to candidates for a variety of reasons that have nothing to do with helping them win elections; in fact, many of the biggest campaign donors prefer to give to candidates whom they expect to win, as certain winners are a better investment for those wanting future access to address policy concerns. Of course, in today's heated battle for control of Congress, competitive races draw more attention from donors on both sides of the partisan divide. As FairVote demonstrated in 2002, the result is that winning percentages in House races are actually negatively correlated with the campaign spending by both winners and losers. In other words, as a candidate spends more and more money, he or she tends to win by smaller and smaller amounts.

For indications that much money isn't being given just to defeat candidates of another party, take two examples from 2000: Pennsylvania-9's Bud Shuster, who spent more than $1.1 million that year, and Arkansas-3's Asa Hutchison, who spent more than $800,000. Their spending levels were above average but otherwise unremarkable—except that both candidates were uncontested and won election with 100% of the vote, safely ensconced in districts secure for their party. Clearly, in these and many other cases, their contributors were betting on a sure thing.

On the other hand, there are many races where the candidates spent similar amounts, but the winner won by more than 20%. Examples from 2000 included Steve Buyer (IN-5), whose opponent spent over $400K compared to Buyer's $330K; Patsy Mink (HI-2), where both candidates spent around $200K; and Tom Allen (ME-1), where Allen and his opponent spent a little more than $350K.

The sharpest decline in competition occurred after the 1996 elections, when no redistricting was happening.

There were three House races that year in which both candidates spent more than $2 million. The candidate who spent more money lost two out of three. Four out of the top five biggest spending losers outspent their opponents. Ten candidates spent more than $2 million in 2000. Five won, and five lost. Of the five losers, four of them outspent their opponents but lost anyway. If spending really determined the outcome of every race—not just who won but by how much—then one would expect to find competitive races when candidates spend similar amounts and lopsided races when one candidate outspends the other. This turns out not to be the case. Instead, the winner and winning percentage is far more closely correlated with the partisanship of the district, which is determined long before candidates start raising and spending money. . . .

It's Not Gerrymandering: The Roots of Non-Competition Run Far Deeper

With rising rates of incumbent retention, lopsided elections and the visceral impact of the Texas re-redistricting in 2003 suggesting to Democrats that Republicans can steal elections through gerrymandering, redistricting processes have drawn increasing attention from reformers and editorial writers. But the bracing reality is that political gerrymandering in 2001–2 only had a minimal impact on overall lack of competition and is not the root cause of the bias toward Republicans that exists in congressional districts. Consider these points:

1. Our elections have been non-competitive for decades, starting well before modern tools of gerrymandering emerged and even before states regularly redistricted at the start of a decade. In 1956, for example, 96% of incumbents won and 95.4% of seats stayed in the same party's hands; indeed at least 88% of incumbents won in every election since 1952, including 99% in 1968, 97% in 1976 and more than 98% in both 1986 and 1988—years when more than 85% of all incumbents won by margins of more than 20%.

2. It is true that we are in the midst of the least competitive congressional elections in history, and certainly one can measure specific means by which certain incumbents were protected in 2001–2002. But the great majority of incumbents did not need nor [did they] receive any help in redistricting. . . . [T]he great bulk of districts were changed by less than 2.5% in partisanship in post-2000 redistricting—207 out of 326 that we analyzed. Another 77 districts had their partisanship shift by between 2.5% and 5.5%, but only 42 districts were changed by more than 5.5%, which is the only kind of change that alone could turn a competitive race into a

landslide win. Yet even in these 42 districts, only 27 of the partisan shifts in redistricting helped the incumbent party.

3. The sharpest decline in competition occurred after the 1996 elections, when no redistricting was happening. The combination of the Cold War ending in 1989, Bill Clinton winning the presidency in 1992 and Republicans taking over the House in 1994 led to a hardening of partisan voting patterns in federal races that contributed to the Republican win in 1994 and a modest Democratic comeback in 1996. But by 1998, the field of play was generally set, with a sharp decline in incumbents representing the opposition party's district. That year, one in which the impeachment of Bill Clinton only further polarized the country, only six House incumbents lost, and fewer than 10% of races were won by less than 10%. We have experienced single-digit incumbent defeat numbers ever since, and the number of races won by less than 10% have never dropped to fewer than nine in ten races. It is true that redistricting typically would have created an upward blip in competition in 2002, but even such a temporary increase in competitive races would have had a minor impact on the overall problem of lack of voter choice.

4. The same dramatic drop in competition has taken place in states in presidential contests decided by the Electoral College—moving from 24 states being in a swing state position in 1976, representing 345 electoral votes, to just 13 similarly defined swing states representing 159 electoral votes in 2004. State lines of course are not redrawn, and major party presidential candidates have great access to the media and to campaign dollars—but none of those factors has stopped the decline in competitive states. FairVote's report, Presidential Election

Inequality, available in hard copy and on-line at
www.fairvote.org/presidential, helps show just how
and why this has occurred.

5. Republicans have a definitive edge in the number of
districts their presidential candidate carries in a nationally even year, but that edge has in fact declined since
the 1970s. Their past advantage was obscured by the fact
that so many House Democrats before 1994 were able to
represent Republican-leaning districts, but a single-
member district's bias against the party whose support
is more concentrated is nothing new. . . .

Redistricting Commissions Will Not Help with Competition

Even if commissions typically are a worthy reform to address
the conflict of interest that comes with politicians helping
their political friends and hurting their enemies, independent
redistricting alone will never achieve a complete set of worthy
public interest goals at the same time: competitive elections,
partisan fairness, racial fairness, geographic coherence and ac-
countable leadership.

Competition, for example, requires districts with a narrow
partisan division, which in turn almost certainly means that
racial minorities will not have the power to consistently elect
candidates of choice as required under the Voting Rights Act.
Competitive districts also pave the way for wild shifts in party
balance despite only small statewide shifts in the vote balance.
And given that most areas have natural partisan leanings,
drawing competitive districts makes it difficult to follow traditional criteria like compactness and maintenance of local political lines.

In part due to these inherent conflicts, independent redistricting has had minimal impact on electoral competition and,
at best, mixed impact on fair partisan, racial and gender representation. Arizona and Iowa are often highlighted by redis-

tricting reformers for having adopted independent redistricting for congressional and state legislative elections, but neither state has particularly competitive elections nor the increased accountability and fairer representation sought by most reformers. In Arizona, for example, 15 of 16 U.S. House races were won by landslide margins of more than 20% in the first two elections since independent redistricting in 2001, and no incumbent has come close to losing. None of its 30 state senate seats were competitive in 2004; indeed almost half were not even contested.

Even though Iowa is almost uniquely balanced in its partisan division across much of the state, all of its U.S. House incumbents in 2004 were re-elected, with an average margin of victory of 18%. Iowa's incumbency rate in fact has been more than 97% since the adoption of independent redistricting. In addition, no woman has been elected to Congress in either Iowa or Arizona since adoption of independent redistricting, and women candidates have fared less well in state elections held after each round of independent redistricting in those states. Arizona Latinos sued their state plan, which has been in continuous litigation since 2002. The reality is that voter choice and fair representation are mutually exclusive in a single-member district, even with independent redistricting. The partisan imbalance within different areas of most states makes it impossible to draw districts that are both reasonably shaped and at the same time competitive.

A Combination of Incumbency, Winner-Take-All Elections, and Hardening Partisanship

As we look at how strikingly non-competitive House elections have become, we must confront the fact that by far the most important factor is that the U.S. House is elected in winner-take-all, single-member districts. Winner-take-all elections held with plurality voting rules tend to limit general elections to candidates from two parties. Given that the great majority of geographically-defined areas in the nation show clear preference for one party over the other, most incumbents have virtually a free ride because their party is preferred in their district. Even in those relatively few districts that are more balanced between backers of the major parties, incumbents can use a variety of advantages that come with their office— such as being quick to respond to constituents' non-partisan needs, sending out regular free mail to district voters, raising large sums of money—to make their defeat nearly impossible without exposure of personal corruption or a major national partisan shift.

Recent years have exaggerated the problem of lack of competition for several reasons: (1) incumbents and parties are more sophisticated about what incumbent officeholders should do in serving their district to shield themselves from competition; (2) new computerized methods of redistricting, combined with the need to draw new districts every ten years and the lack of nonpartisan standards governing the process, increasing the number of districts with a partisan tilt; (3) those partisan tilts are more decisive than ever because the national parties have become quite distinct in most voters' minds, leading to less ticket-splitting.

Most congressional districts are going to be non-competitive no matter how the district lines are drawn.

The end result is that most voters don't have a choice between two candidates, let alone three—so much for a healthy two-party system, where issues ignored by one major party can be meaningfully addressed by the other one. If voters would like to hear about the policy ideas of independent and third party candidates, they are even more shut out. Yes, voter turnout is down over recent decades, but we believe it is time to stop blaming the victims of the American electoral system—the voters—and start addressing the root causes of alienation and lack of representation: our winner-take-all electoral system, buttressed by incumbent privileges and, yes, campaign cash and partisan redistricting run amok.

Reform Lessons from Partisan Voting Patterns in U.S. House Races, 1972–2002

If one studies the shifting district partisanship in congressional districts over recent decades, two trends stand out:

- Republican presidential candidates consistently run ahead of their national average in a large majority of districts (that measure is the consistent one we use to determine whether a district has a Republican bias or Democratic national bias).

- Democratic Party dominance of districts with a Democratic bias has been relatively consistent over time—and the total number of such seats in fact has increased. Republican growth in House seats has come heavily in seats with a Republican bias.

We believe these facts support our contention that much of the behavior of legislators in Congress and the greater entrenchment of more incumbents are founded on the parties becoming more distinct and on voters voting more on national perceptions of the parties.

Because most congressional district-sized geographic areas have clear partisan tilts, then most congressional districts are going to be non-competitive no matter how the district lines are drawn. Redistricting reform certainly could make an incremental improvement in competitive choice, but potentially at a cost to representation of racial minorities. In contrast, by adopting a version of the Illinois model for electing its state house of representatives used from 1870 to 1980 (a non-winner-take-all system in three-seat legislative districts), nearly every three-seat constituency would have two-party representation as well as competition within parties in the general election. Representatives would cover the left, center and right of the spectrum in greater balance than now. Racial minorities would have opportunities to elect seats in more areas of the nation, and women would be more likely to run and win. Instructively, in 2001, a bipartisan panel in Illinois led by former Congressman Abner Mikva and former Illinois Governor Jim Edgar recommended restoring the Illinois model in order to achieve better elections and governance.

3

Electronic Voting Is Inherently Flawed and Vulnerable to Fraud

Wendy M. Grossman

Wendy M. Grossman has written about the Internet and related technologies for numerous publications.

Voting machines are inherently flawed and susceptible to fraud. Although incidents of glitches in these machines are reported, officials continue to use them. One of the better-known manufacturers of voting machines, Diebold, has had problems with not only voting machines, but also automatic teller machines (ATM). In both cases a major flaw is that the machines use a "black box" recorder; once you vote there is no way to prove or disprove how you voted, and a similar problem exists with ATM withdrawals. Although voter fraud can lead to costly lawsuits, the real victims in this system are the voters.

It's commonly said that insanity is doing the same thing over and over again while expecting different results. Yet this is what we keep doing with electronic voting machines— find flaws and try again. It should therefore have been no surprise when, at the end of March [2009], California's secretary of state's office of voting system technology assessment decertified older voting systems from Diebold's Premier Election Solutions division. The reason: a security flaw that erased 197 votes in the Humboldt county precinct in last November's [2008] presidential election.

Wendy M. Grossman, "Why Machines Are Bad at Counting Votes," *Guardian*, April 30, 2009. Reproduced by permission of Guardian News Service, LTD.

Clearly, 197 votes would not have changed the national result. But the loss, which exceeds the error rate allowed under
the Help America Vote Act of 2002, was only spotted because
a local citizen group, the Humboldt County Election Transparency Project (humtp.com) monitored the vote using a
ballot-imaging scanner to create an independent record. How
many votes were lost elsewhere?

---

*How much time have you got to test that a given voting
system will function perfectly under all possible circumstances?*

Humboldt county used Diebold's GEMS operating system
version 1.18.19 to tally postal ballots scanned in batches, or
"decks". The omission of votes was a result of a flaw in the
system, where, given particular circumstances, it deletes the
first deck, named "Deck Zero", without noting it in the system's
audit logs.

Voting Slips

Diebold recommended decertification of its older version,
which should force precincts to upgrade and eliminate the
flaw. But the secretary of state's report notes flaws in the audit
logs that will be harder to erase: wrongly recorded entry dates
and times, and silent deletions of audit logs.

"It's nothing new," says Rebecca Mercuri, a security consultant who studied voting systems for her 1999 doctoral dis-
sertation. "These are all security flaws that are well known in
the industry. Why are they acting as if this is the first time
they've heard this?" The audit log problems were documented
in Bev Harris's 2004 book, *Black Box Voting*.

Mercuri explains that election software belongs to the class
of problems known as "NP-complete", that is, problems computers cannot solve in a known amount of time. How much

time have you got to test that a given voting system will function perfectly under all possible circumstances?

"What are people going to do about it?" she asks. "Say we fixed it when it's theoretically not possible to fix these things at any real level?"

So, it's not fair just to pick on Diebold. Last month, election officials in Clay county, Kentucky, were charged with conspiring to alter ballots cast on ES&S iVotronic election machines in recent elections. The key: interface design. In most cases, voters cast ballots by pressing a big red button labelled "VOTE". But some versions of the system require touching a "confirm vote" box on the screen to complete the ballot. It is alleged officials hid this fact from voters and would then "correct" and confirm the ballot after the voter had left. The officials have pleaded not guilty.

Matt Blaze, a security researcher at the University of Pennsylvania, writes in his blog that if this were a strategy, "it's a pretty elegant attack, exploiting little more than a poorly designed, ambiguous user interface, printed instructions that conflict with actual machine behaviour, and public unfamiliarity with equipment that most citizens use at most once or twice each year. And once done, it leaves behind little forensic evidence to expose the deed."

But Diebold's current problems aren't limited to voting machines. More startling was the discovery of malware designed to attack its ATMs. Graham Cluley, a senior technology consultant for the security company Sophos, says the company found a sample in its archives.

"If [the malware] were planted on the version of Windows on those Diebold machines," Cluley says, "you could actually steal information from the cards being used on the device, and hackers with a specially crafted card would get a receipt with people's information." Diebold sent out a customer warning in January and provided a software update.

As in the Kentucky voting machine case, the attack on Diebold's ATMs requires inside access. "We're seeing more and more organised criminal gangs because of the money they can make," says Cluley, pointing out how difficult it would be to spot a legitimate maintenance engineer who's been bought off installing an extra patch off a USB stick in a back pocket.

Black Box Recorder

For consumers, the problem is that both ATMs and voting machines are black-box technologies. You can count your cash and keep the receipt; but if someone else withdrew the money you can't prove it wasn't you. "It's the same with voting," Mercuri says. "You have no way to prove or disprove how you voted."

At least with voting, citizen groups are motivated to push for greater transparency. Jason Kitcat, Green councillor for Brighton and Hove, organised volunteers to observe e-voting trials in the 2007 local government elections in England and Scotland on behalf of the Open Rights Group.

"We saw the same audit log issues," he says. "We know from a computer science point of view that making an audit log that can't be changed is impossible. But it seems as if there's a huge disconnect between people who are computer-science literate, and the people delivering the policy."

Besides, politicians like making uncontroversial decisions. Who could fault them for trusting a company that makes ATMs worldwide? Again, it comes back to humans.

"The folks who buy ATMs [bank managers] and voting machines [election officials] don't really want to pay for a facility that will make it easier for people to challenge them," says Ross Anderson, a professor of security engineering at Cambridge University.

"In the long run, of course, this ends up costing them more: fraud can lead to challenges that are systemic rather than local. Nevertheless, the purchasers may be rational. Most of the bank managers who bought crap ATM systems in the 80s are retired now—they got away with it. With voting machines, some vendors have been discredited in some countries, but lots of money has still been made."

That is, from us—the taxpayer and the bank customer. Kitcat says: "It is shocking that in this day and age this has been allowed to continue."

4

Electronic Voting Can Be Made Secure Against Fraud and Human Error

Paul Venezia

Paul Venezia is a consultant and a senior contributing editor for InfoWorld, *an online information technology magazine.*

During the past decade, the failures of voting machines and mechanisms have become more urgent than the elections themselves. However, little has changed: the development of "e-voting" technology is still closed to all but a few proprietary vendors— including the maker of the most problematic voting machine. In order to solve the array of technical problems and obstacles— from defective memory cartridges to the lack of a paper trail— e-voting should become open source, wherein numerous vendors freely build upon and improve existing systems, software, and devices. This would allow information technology experts to bring their innovations to the polls, reducing the margins for human error and fraud.

"It is enough that the people know there was an election. The people who cast the votes decide nothing. The people who count the votes decide everything."—Joseph Stalin

In the past eight years [2000 to 2008], elections in the United States have taken on the guise of a TV game show, with the elections themselves not quite as compelling as watch-

Paul Venezia, "Open Source: How E-Voting Should Be Done," *InfoWorld*, October 27, 2008. Republished with permission of InfoWorld Media Group, conveyed through Copyright Clearance Center, Inc.

ing voting mechanisms fail across the country, especially in key battleground states such as Florida and Ohio. Pols and pundits from both sides of the aisle are quick to place most of the blame on faulty electronic voting systems. But until we set a technical policy that favors open voting systems, as Australia did in 2001 with its open source eVACS (Electronic Voting and Counting System), we have only ourselves to blame.

The Closed Source Approach to Disenfranchisement

Current U.S. policy ensures that e-voting remains in the hands of very few proprietary vendors, including the much-maligned Diebold, which has received so much bad press that it has re-named its voting machine division Premier Election Solutions.

Don't let the new name fool you. Little has changed about e-voting systems, which take on several forms, including the two most common: touchscreen devices and optical-scan read-ers. What they have in common, however, is that they all use closed source code [proprietary software with restrictions re-garding its use and modifications]. In many cases, even the manufacturers don't have the source code to software running on their own systems. Premier Election Solutions recently ad-vised that its machines lost votes in Ohio primaries due to an incompatibility with McAfee's anti-virus software. In the words of XKCD [an online comic strip], someone is clearly doing their job horribly wrong. Later, Premier claimed that its own software was at fault.

More often than not, however, blame for e-voting failure is placed on the storage media of these devices, either due to their relative fragility or their apparent ease of tampering.

When results from elections conducted on e-voting sys-tems are called into question, manufacturers point the finger at defective "memory cartridges." Those of us in IT [informa-tion technology] know that if all flash storage were this error-prone, digital cameras and iPods wouldn't exist. Worse, we know it's far simpler to pocket or swap out a small flash card containing a few thousand votes than it would be if those votes were recorded on paper ballots.

Another problem of current e-voting systems is that many still in operation provide no paper trail. Americans can't fill up their cars or access their bank accounts from an ATM without being prompted to print a receipt, but in many voting precincts, we can vote with nothing tangible to show for it.

Most voters already know these systems are flawed. It's the relative lack of outrage that is troubling. Perhaps trust in the electoral process is still sufficient to assuage fears of stolen elections, or the issue of flawed voting technology itself has become a running joke, like cracks about an honest politician. Even *The Simpsons* parodied the situation recently.

Those of us who live in IT every day know better. We know exactly how poorly designed some software frameworks are. We see the security challenges presented by Web servers, mail servers, remote access, and so on, but when it comes to the foundation of our democracy, we just shake our heads and move on.

This being a free-market economy, vendors should certainly be able to participate in the construction of truly secure e-voting systems.

Maybe it's time for us geeks to come to the rescue, with a little help from Congress. We've built the Internet, designed staggeringly complex technologies for conducting lightning-speed financial transactions, securing sensitive patient data, even our own entertainment. After all, you'd be hard-pressed to say that there's more complexity in an e-voting machine than in, say, your TiVo or even your cell phone.

But the key to securing e-voting resides in making its systems open source.

Opening the Polls to Open Source

If you look around the open source community, you will find a wide variety of projects that are not only widely used but extremely well designed and very secure. Apache, Perl, PHP, OpenBSD, FreeBSD, and the Linux kernel are just a few examples. Coders who contribute to these projects generally do so without remuneration, producing some of the best code available.

It's time for us to make good on the promise of open elections and open our e-voting systems as well—no black boxes, no intellectual property protections, no obfuscation [intentionally making communication confusing], and certainly no backdoors. Doing so would require a federal mandate, one that would eliminate the use of closed source devices.

This being a free-market economy, vendors should certainly be able to participate in the construction of truly secure e-voting systems. But to ensure the integrity of our elections, the code they run on their products must be open. Moreover, it should be the same across all e-voting platforms. Just as the PC industry produces multiple PC brands that all run Windows, e-voting vendors should produce systems that run the same open source voting software.

The open source community has already gotten involved in reshaping our approach to e-voting systems. The Open Voting Consortium, for example, is pushing for simple, standard touchscreen voting systems that do not directly interface with any system, or record votes. These systems would simply print paper voting receipts with bar codes that would then be scanned and dropped into a ballot box, officially casting the vote.

This method removes the need for any polling station to be held responsible for counting votes, thus eliminating any effect tampering with machines might have on results. It also ensures a paper trail for potential recounts. Moreover, by relying on paper in printers rather than official ballots, no voter can be turned away for lack of ballots at a polling place.

This solution is cheap and straightforward, yet isn't widely used. Instead, we have spent billions of dollars on commercial solutions that offer no paper trail—just a poor security history.

One recent example involved a Republican at-large election in Washington, D.C., in which thousands of votes appeared and then disappeared during the day. Sequoia Voting Systems equipment was used for that election. Not surprisingly, Sequoia has laid the blame for those phantom votes on human error, perhaps a corrupt memory cartridge. Retailers wouldn't accept cash registers that were this error-prone. In many cases, brand-new e-voting systems have been shelved due to such issues, at a fantastic cost to taxpayers.

Network Integrity: Ensuring All Votes Count

Leveraging existing network infrastructures to completely remove the polling place from the vote-counting equation is another essential step to ensuring secure elections.

In many cases, public polling is conducted in government buildings, schools, community centers, and other facilities equipped with some form of broadband Internet access. Devices running open source software could be made to create an instant, encrypted link to transmit all votes to a centralized server, while still providing a paper trail at the polling place in the form of a printout.

In this way, votes from a significant number of precincts could be counted as they are entered, rather than after the fact. Communication with the central server would be secured using existing encryption methods such as AES (Advanced Encryption Standard) and certificate-based authentication.

Even when voting in someone's garage, your vote would be more secure than it would be using a pile of flash cards in a box.

In addition, these devices wouldn't require manual configuration. Once connected and authenticated to the central server, all ballot choices would be pulled from the central server for display to the voter. Thus, setting up the polling place would simply require volunteers to plug everything in and turn the systems on.

The ability to view the code that records our votes should be a basic right.

Of course, connectivity to the central server is sure to be this solution's weakest link. Though all transactions would be encrypted, the system would also need to incorporate a queuing method to retain votes until the server is available. This functionality could also maintain vote integrity even where Internet connectivity is not available. Simply connect the device to the network at a later time, and the votes are delivered to the central server. As above, paper receipts of each vote would be made available as they were cast, as a fallback should problems occur.

Open Source in the Voting Booth

Anyone familiar with current e-voting technologies will note that the logistics of this solution are no more or less complex than those of existing systems. The key, however, is that they would be driven by open source code that anyone could download and use.

With all the covers off, it becomes extremely difficult to embed backdoors or commit cloak-and-dagger fraud. The ability to view the code that records our votes should be a basic right—if only to ensure that the conditions leading to a successfully recorded vote do not set success as a default.

The best bet for an open voting system would be code based on NetBSD or OpenBSD, embedded in nonremovable flash on the mainboard of the device. The device would also require a serial or USB-driven touchscreen, as well as a USB-connected, embedded printer. Code updates to the device would not be allowed via the touchscreen, but rather through a certificate or key-secured USB or serial connection.

Such a device would be less complex than a McDonald's cash register, running extremely basic, open code that's been hardened for years, and can be easily reduced to only the required functions. There's no reason it couldn't be cheap, simple, and extremely easy to produce. Further, it should easily handle being mothballed for a year or two between elections.

Detractors will claim that if the code is open, anyone planning to commit fraud will have the blueprints to circumvent the security of the system. The ever-growing adoption of open source software in businesses large and small, as well as the Internet's reliance on open source solutions, provides evidence to the contrary. For example, open cryptography solutions are no less secure than their closed counterparts. In fact, one could argue that they're more secure, given that complete code visibility greatly reduces the potential for backdoors.

Open Elections Require Open Systems

Ultimately, the call for open source e-voting systems isn't as much about open source software as it is about securing our inalienable right to legitimate elections. It just so happens that open source is the best way to accomplish that goal.

If the past few elections are any indication, secure voting machines are essential to political legitimacy. With machines sold by companies that produce far more secure ATMs than voting systems, something must change, especially as the inaccuracies and irregularities incurred by these systems continue to mount. No effective steps have been taken by the government thus far to address the integrity of our vote, other than small measures by state and county governments that have already blown budgets on insecure systems.

From banking to taxes to tollbooths, computers ostensibly provide a dispassionate third party to tally numbers, not as we might wish them to be but as they are.

In 2002, Congress passed the Help America Vote Act in response to the hanging-chad debacle of Florida's 2000 presidential elections. The act's main thrust was to provide money to states to replace outdated punch-card- and lever-based voting systems with optical-scan or touchscreen models. The act largely accomplished that goal, filling the coffers of closed source voting system manufacturers. In doing so, the act may have inadvertently placed the country in a worse situation, given how difficult it is to rig large numbers of votes with punch card or lever systems. By contrast, a single poorly designed e-voting machine can be used to covertly modify large numbers of votes.

Of course, even with a paper ballot cast in a locked box, there have never been fail-safe assurances that any given vote has been counted and recorded. Human error and malfeasance are sure to be constants.

Yet in every industry, computers have reduced or eliminated human error and guarded against fraud. From banking to taxes to tollbooths, computers ostensibly provide a dispassionate third party to tally numbers, not as we might wish them to be but as they are. Voting systems are no exception, and they should be afforded far more protections, oversight, and regulation than those in most other industries as they protect the very foundation for our democracy.

The law has always trailed behind technical innovation. In the case of e-voting, Congress must act to close this gap, by passing legislation to provide grants for developing a single, open framework for all voting systems and to provide funds to states to retrofit existing hardware where possible.

This "Open Vote Act" should also enact laws that prohibit the use of any voting system that does not provide a paper audit trail, and it should mandate that companies use government-approved voting code without modification when building proprietary systems. If we can nationalize big banks and spend a trillion dollars to recover from the irresponsible actions of a relative few, we can certainly nationalize portions of our voting infrastructure. There's too much at risk to think otherwise.

Hanlon's Razor: Information Technology's Call to Action

As we head into the 2008 elections, we all hope that there are no surprises come Election Day. The media will hang on every instance of voting-system inaccuracy, and we're sure to hear from voters across the country who have been inadvertently disenfranchised by malfunctioning e-voting systems.

Here, Hanlon's razor ("Never attribute to malice that which can be adequately explained by stupidity.") comes into play. If there are widespread problems with e-voting systems this time around, we have no one but ourselves to blame. We have seen the flaws of these systems, and we have not acted to correct the system that has given rise to them.

If voting irregularities occur during this election, let's hope the novelty of current e-voting systems will wear off for the population at large, giving way to meaningful voting reform in Washington. If everything seems to go smoothly, however, let's not just assume the issue of e-voting security has magically gone away.

Either way, those of us who know how computers work, who know how easy it is to slip backdoors into closed code, and who know how these problems should be addressed will always provide an undercurrent of distrust—not just for our individual votes but for the entire elections system in general.

Isn't it time we put our knowledge into action?

5

Use of Mail and Absentee Ballots Is Increasing

Sam Rosenfeld

Sam Rosenfeld is a former Web editor for American Prospect, *a liberal political magazine.*

The vote-by-mail system established in Oregon is gaining public support and extensive adoption throughout the nation. Combined with the legislative call for election reform and the pitfalls and stresses of operating electronic voting machines, registrars and election officials from various states gradually are turning to vote-by-mail and absentee ballots, which are simpler, cheaper, and more secure. Critics allege that such methods are subject to fraud, such as impersonation and vote buying, and that allowing voters to cast their ballots early removes them from late-breaking, critical election developments. Nevertheless, Oregon and other vote-by-mail states have not reported wide-scale fraud or voter discontent.

Oregon's statewide vote-by-mail system remains unique—for now. But with little fanfare, liberalized absentee balloting laws elsewhere have prompted a steady expansion of mail voting. In the process, popular support is growing, from the ground up. States are following the gradualist pattern of expansion first set in Oregon. Laws permitting at-will absentee registration in dozens of states, and permanent absentee registration policies in California and elsewhere, are expanding the pool of voters who know and like the process.

Sam Rosenfeld, "On the Oregon Trail," *American Prospect*, April 14, 2006. Reproduced with permission from The American Prospect, 11 Beacon St., Suite 1120, Boston, MA 02108.

Meanwhile, in Arizona, Colorado, and Washington, municipalities and counties have won the option to run all vote-by-mail elections for various contests. More local election administrators are opting for mail balloting to save money and simplify the process. Oregon eventually reached a tipping point of popular support that pushed the entire state to vote by mail; most observers think Washington state has now reached the same point, and other western states are close behind.

This election year may turn out to be the catalytic moment for the expansion of mail voting. Pressure from looming Help America Vote Act (HAVA) and state-level compliance requirements, combined with the continued headaches associated with implementing and securing electronic voting systems, are provoking registrars and election officials in many states to advocate switching to a system that simplifies the process, saves money, and addresses major logistical and security concerns. Meanwhile, for the first time, advocates are organizing nationally and providing cross-state support and coordination for efforts to spread mail voting. Given the ground-level trends, vote-by-mail proponents feel the wind at their backs.

Electoral Quakes

California represents the biggest and least noticed expansion of absentee balloting. The turning point for the Golden State was 2001's enactment of permanent no-excuse absentee voting. Between 2002 and 2005, use of mail voting shot up statewide by more than a million votes, with absentee ballots accounting for 27 percent of votes cast in 2002, 33 percent in 2004, and 40 percent in 2005's special election. As use has expanded especially quickly in liberal counties, absentee voting's traditional Republican tilt has diminished. (The GOP [Republican]-Democratic share of the absentee ballot vote was 47 to 41 percent in 1992; in 2005 it was 41 to 41 percent.)

While voters value the convenience, registrars actively encourage absentee voting to relieve administrative costs. "The voters are flocking to voting by mail in droves," reports Elaine Ginnold, registrar of voters for Alameda County, population 1.5 million, which includes the cities of Berkeley and Oakland. Absentee ballots accounted for 36 percent of Alameda's votes in 2004 and 47 percent in 2005's special election.

A state law passed in 2004 requires that electronic machines be equipped with paper trail printers for contemporaneous ballot verification by the voter. Counties across California had already procured machines that lacked such printers, and this year [2006] the secretary of state's office took too long to certify new machines for several counties to complete the procurement process in time for June. ("It's $12.7 million down the toilet," remarks Ginnold, referring to 4,000 noncompliant Diebold machines sitting in a warehouse in Alameda County.) Meanwhile, a lawsuit filed this year by California voters and activists seeking to block use of Diebold equipment in the June primary reflects the continued unease electronic machines inspire among significant numbers of voters.

Absentee ballots could well surpass 50 percent of the total California vote share in November. Ginnold sees 60 percent mail voting—which California might reach by the 2008 election—as a tipping point, when popular support will finally prompt either a ballot initiative to make the state all vote by mail or the reticent state legislature to give counties the option to run all-vote-by-mail elections. Either option, Ginnold says, would lead to universal vote by mail statewide. "I think what happened in Oregon is eventually going to happen here."

Going National

Oregon's neighbor to the north, meanwhile, is set to attain all vote-by-mail status imminently, having granted counties the option of choosing comprehensive vote by mail. Permanent-registration absentee balloting was first introduced in Washington state for disabled and elderly voters in the mid-1980s. It was expanded as an option for all voters, with no excuse required, early in the 1990s. "Many counties started having 75 to 85 percent of their voters choosing it," recalls Sam Reed, Washington's Republican secretary of state and a longtime proponent of vote by mail. "So last year I requested a bill to allow counties to exercise an option to go all vote by mail."

So far 34 out of 39 counties have opted for the system, and King County, encompassing Seattle and a full third of the state's registered voters, will likely do so by mid-2007. Most observers predict the remaining four counties will follow suit, and that by 2008, Washington will be the second state in the country to conduct all statewide elections by mail.

Until this year, no national advocacy outfit existed to help accelerate such absentee voting trends and leverage them to boost support for all-vote-by-mail systems. Political consultant Adam J. Smith has stepped into the organizational breach with the Portland-based Vote By Mail Project. Oregon Secretary of State Bill Bradbury serves on its board, and the outfit receives institutional and financial backing from the National Association of Letter Carriers (for obvious reasons, a major proponent of mail voting).

"We're going to support the whole continuum of vote by mail," says Smith, "from no excuse permanent absentee registration, to county option vote by mail, to statewide vote by mail. The natural progression seems to be you need to introduce the issue to people and give them the opportunity to vote this way, and inevitably the majority of people will decide they like it better." States in his sights include not only California but also Arizona, Colorado, and New Mexico—all places where liberalized absentee laws have sparked expanded use of mail balloting in recent years. Meanwhile, the recently formed Progressive Legislative Action Network is also planning to push for liberalized absentee and universal vote-by-mail laws.

Recorders in Arizona's two biggest counties estimate that 60 percent of their ballots for the 2006 midterms will be cast by mail. Phoenix and Tucson will also be holding all-vote-by-mail local elections. Meanwhile, a movement to put a state-wide vote-by-mail initiative on the 2006 ballot was born when Rick Murphy, an Arizona Republican businessman, lost a congressional primary challenge in 2004 to Christian right darling Trent Franks. "It became quite obvious to Rick that the system was broken," says Fred Taylor, state director of Your Right to Vote and Murphy's partner in the vote-by-mail ballot initiative. "With a very small minority of the voters, you can win a primary election when there's such a low turnout. Rick wants to see a system that boosts engagement and dilutes the power of interest groups."

Overall, the process of implementing the [direct recording electronic voting] system in localities across the country has been marred by more difficulties than most could have imagined.

It's still early to gauge Murphy and Taylor's prospects in Arizona, but Colorado's experience in 2002 amply illustrates the pitfalls of moving too quickly for statewide change. That year, Democrat Rutt Bridges campaigned for a ballot initiative to make the entire state all vote by mail at a time when counties did not have the option to use the system and voters generally lacked experience with it. Like the majority of ballot initiatives on any issue in any election, it failed. Bridges now reflects that states should follow a more gradualist strategy for achieving vote by mail, something Colorado has demonstrated since the 2002 loss. . . .

Electronic Hell

Thirty states have spent more than $300 million since 2002 in federal funds to replace punch-card and lever machines with updated voting technology. Certainly there are places where the shift to direct recording electronic (DRE) systems occurred early, went smoothly, and met with general public satisfaction. And, as defenders of electronic voting technology like Ohio State's Daniel Tokaji emphasize, DRE machines do constitute a net improvement over punch-card and lever voting in terms of promoting accessibility and lowering miscount rates. But overall, the process of implementing the system in localities across the country has been marred by more difficulties than most could have imagined, contributing to a debilitating crisis of public confidence in electronic voting technology.

A 2004 North Carolina election for state agricultural commissioner, which collapsed in the wake of a major DRE programming glitch in Carteret County, served as a rallying cry for critics of electronic voting. Last December [2005], election officials and computer experts in Florida's Leon County tested machines provided by Diebold and showed that election results could be manipulated from within the Elections Office with relative ease—and with no one knowing. Diebold responded by cutting off any communication with the county elections supervisor who'd instigated the test. Primary elections this March [2006] in Texas and Illinois, where DRE machines were used for the first time on a large scale in many localities, were the latest to be marred by major glitches in the tabulations, due to both machine errors and inadequate pollworker training.

Also in March, Maryland made the stunning decision to dump its $90 million investment in Diebold machines due to the lack of a paper-auditing trail that could facilitate recounts. The paper-trail issue is a key fulcrum for organized resistance to electronic technology. Twenty-five states now have requirements for voter-verified paper audit trails (VVPAT) like the one in California, which are provoking major bureaucratic complications as officials attempt to graft printing technologies on to pre-existing electronic machines.

Problems with compliance provide the context for lawsuits against electronic voting machine vendors in five states beyond California. Meanwhile, a lobbying coalition of DRE skeptics gathered on Capitol Hill the first week of April [2006] to push for Democrat Rush Holt's bill mandating VVPAT for all electronic machines, programming that allows for independent audits, and hand-counted verification for 2 percent of all ballots cast.

HAVA Heart

As Tokaji himself has demonstrated, grafting VVPAT technology onto existing electronic systems is not only proving to be cumbersome and logistically problematic, it also doesn't provide the panacea to security concerns that advocates think it does. VVPAT provisions heighten the complexity of the voting process, and hand-count audits of select ballots have proven to be enormously time-consuming for election officials in places like Nevada, where it has been attempted.

Unfortunately, the response to these dilemmas by many election experts and consultants, invested as they are in the push to "make HAVA work," has been to try to reform electronic voting by plunging ever deeper into the logistical weeds of DRE compliance. Speaking at an American University conference on election reform held in late March [2006], Tokaji listed at least four different teams of researchers and consultants, spanning various universities as well as the National Science Foundation and the National Academy of Sciences, who would be monitoring the 2006 elections and proposing further reforms.

HAVA has spawned a whole techno-academic-industrial complex. At the same conference, voting security expert Avi Rubin of ACCURATE (A Center for Correct, Usable, Reliable, Auditable, and Transparent Elections) proposed a truly daunting array of new reforms to ensure the integrity of electronic voting, from rendering all electronic systems interoperable and their coding open source, to mandating regular "threat analysis, code review, architectural analysis, and penetration testing"—so as to ensure that the system "can be trusted to the same degree as critical military, medical, and banking systems."

But this endless regress, reminiscent of *Mad Magazine*'s "Spy vs. Spy," may only be leading experts and officials deeper into electronic Rube Goldberg[1] territory and further away from the basic election reform principles HAVA was meant to address in the first place. And this reality is a big part of the context for the expansion in the ranks of officials and voters on the ground, in state after state, who are coming to prefer a simpler, lower-tech balloting method—snail mail.

Back to the Future

The local and county-level stirrings in Colorado, Arizona, and California are precisely what the Vote by Mail Project hopes to identify and catalyze nationally. But chicken-and-egg questions about process and political culture linger: Does vote by mail work in Oregon and Washington because it's a universally desirable system or because the Pacific Northwest's historic tradition of clean elections allows it to work? Is vote by mail a desirable alternative for, say, a state like Ohio or Illinois—or might it provide new opportunities for fraud and suppression in states lacking clean civic cultures?

There's no real consensus among election experts on this question, but the record of expanded mail balloting in California, Colorado, and elsewhere is virtually free of fraud or major glitches. Leading critics of mail voting, like Curtis Gans, director of the Committee for the Study of the American Electorate, cite the heightened potential for vote buying in the

---

1. American cartoonist and engineer known for drawing complicated machines that completed simple functions.

mail-voting process, given the lack of a truly secret ballot. (Gans can, indeed, point to a local vote-buying scandal involving absentee ballots in 2003 city elections in northern Indiana.) But Oregon, Washington, and California have not reported any vote-buying incidents during the years that vote-by-mail use has expanded there, and sustaining such fraud on a large scale without detection would likely be prohibitively difficult. Moreover, to the extent such dangers and potential unknowns remain troubling, the gradual, locality-by-locality expansion of vote by mail thus far will help observers detect problems and make proper adjustments *before* a system is implemented across the board in a given state. "We're not comparing this against 'the perfect system'—that doesn't exist," [political consultant] Adam [J.] Smith points out. "Possible problems that might arise can be addressed through best practices."

Proponents note the procedural safeguards built into the Oregon system—most importantly a full registry of digitized signatures that election officials cross-check against voters' signatures on ballot envelopes—that neither exist in the traditional system nor depend for their effectiveness on the honesty and civic virtue of voters. "There are a number of ways to make vote by mail more secure than polling places," says Ann Martens, Secretary of State Bradbury's communications director in Oregon. "Our county elections officials are trained by former state police forensics experts in handwriting analysis . . . [The signature cross-checking] goes through a number of levels where it's either accepted or we eventually contact the voter."

Indeed, the time and ability that vote by mail affords officials to actually contact voters about questionable ballots address a more typical progressive election concern than voter fraud—the prospect of indirect voter suppression by politicized election officials applying deliberately onerous standards to targeted demographics. What if a vote-by-mail official in, say, Ohio, was tempted to reject a significant number of ballots on spurious grounds that the envelope signature didn't match the digitized registration signature? "Checking the signatures is such a process, involving so many workers, it would be really hard to do something like that," says Smith. "Even if you could systematically weed out certain groups, all you're going to do at that point is not in fact disqualify those ballots but force people to prove that they're actually who they say they are. So there are ways to safeguard against that."

Gradual, locality-by-locality expansion of vote by mail thus far will help observers detect problems and make proper adjustments before a system is implemented across the board in a given state.

Advocates hasten to highlight the real-world polling-place scenarios that have played out in elections past, where perfectly legal neglect and shortchanging of resources on the part of election officials led to logistical bottlenecks in various localities—leading, in effect, to de facto voter suppression. The prospects of such Ohio-style scenarios recurring in future elections would be eliminated with vote by mail—as would the dangers, posed by electronic voting, of a logistical screw up or security breach without the capacity for a recount.

Another criticism of vote-by-mail systems (also voiced in opposition to early voting provisions) is that the greatly expanded period for voting leads to "differentials in knowledge" among voters. Some might send in their ballot a week and a half prior to Election Day, and an ensuing dramatic event or development may change the dynamics of the race, leaving those early voters unable to change their decisions. But any voting date, whether it lasts one day or two weeks, is arbitrary, and may occur immediately prior to major occurrences that would have changed the electoral result in retrospect. And to the extent that a longer period for voting discourages the late-

breaking artificial gimmickry and vicissitudes of political campaigns (as transmuted through media narratives and political
advertising), that's more of a plus than a minus. Certainly
Oregon's experience hasn't shown much voter discontent with
the time differentials in voting, just as the state's experience
hasn't revealed any major problems with fraud or logistics.
Nor have citizens among the swelling ranks of mail voters in
states outside of Oregon.

Indeed, the movement for mail voting represents a striking
reversal in a nation that has always been infatuated with new
technology. It is proceeding through firsthand experience,
county by county, voter by voter, in a fascinating democratic
rebellion against both the traditional complications of poll-
site voting as well as insecurities associated with newfangled
electronic technology imposed from above.

6

Mail and Absentee Ballots Are Vulnerable to Fraud

John C. Fortier

John C. Fortier is a research fellow at the American Enterprise Institute for Public Policy Research (AEI), which is based in Washington, D.C.

Absentee and mail ballots are instrumental to several types of voters, such as military personnel stationed abroad, the incapacitated, and travelers. But states should be cautioned against promoting absentee and mail voting. Outside of the polls, voters are at risk of coercion and loss of privacy and such votes are not subjected to error checks. In addition, mail ballots are more susceptible to fraud and interception—including bogus requests for absentee ballots and discarded votes—and do not substantially increase election turnout. Options for absentee and mail voting should not be expanded, and election officials must improve the ways in which these ballots are cast and accounted for.

Voting before election day has become increasingly common in America. In 2004, nearly one quarter of all voters voted before November 2nd, with the majority of those voters casting their votes by absentee ballot.

Access to absentee ballots is essential for several classes of people who really need them, overseas military voters, the bedridden, and travelers, to name a few. But many states have

John C. Fortier, "Expanding and Improving Opportunities to Vote by Mail or Absentee," October 22, 2007. Reprinted with permission of the American Enterprise Institute for Public Policy Research, Washington, D.C. Originally delivered before the Committee on House Administration, Elections Subcommittee.

encouraged the use of absentee voting for those who could otherwise go to the polls. I would like to sound a cautionary note regarding this trend. Casting an absentee ballot, while necessary for some, is inferior to casting a vote at a polling place for two major reasons.

Absentee voting opens up additional opportunities for election fraud.

First, at a polling place, a voter casts a private ballot. By contrast, there is no privacy curtain around an absentee ballot; it has left the protections of the polling place behind. Without privacy protections, absentee voters are susceptible to coercion of their votes. If a voter at a polling place has been pressured by his employer, union, church, community or spouse, he can draw the curtain, vote privately, and thumb his nose at the pressure. With an absentee ballot, voters might not have a choice but to show the filled out ballot to their tormentors or to receive fifty dollars for a ballot "well filled out."

Second, absentee ballots provide greater opportunities for election fraud. Election fraud is very hard to measure, and there are numerous points in the voting process where fraud could occur. But absentee voting opens up additional opportunities for election fraud. Absentee ballots have been fraudulently requested or intercepted in the mail, for example. The most famous instance of absentee voter fraud occurred in the Miami mayoral race in 1998. A court found such irregularities in the absentee ballots, that all absentee ballots were thrown out, which changed the outcome of the election.

There are two additional reasons to be cautious about the expansion of absentee ballot beyond those who need it. First, absentee ballots are not subject to the same error checking as most ballots cast at polling places. There is no solid body of academic research on error rates of absentee ballots compared to ballots cast at a polling place. But there is the simple fact that voters who vote on Optiscan or DRE [direct recording electronic] voting machines will be warned if they have not cast a ballot for a particular race, or they will be warned or prevented from voting for two candidates and thereby invalidating their ballot. Absentee voters have no such check against ballot errors. If an absentee voter, for example, inadvertently votes for two candidates, then that vote cannot be counted. A Cal Tech/MIT [California Institute of Technology/Massachusetts Institute of Technology] study after the 2000 election found that several million ballots for president were invalidated because they had been cast improperly, and subsequently added error checking mechanisms have reduced that number substantially.

A vote cast in advance for a candidate who makes a last minute gaffe cannot be retrieved.

Second, absentee balloting extends the voting period from one day to over a month. Not only does this dilute the civic spirit of a single election day, it also opens up the possibility that the voter will cast a ballot before important information becomes available. A vote cast in advance for a candidate who makes a last minute gaffe cannot be retrieved. In many instances, absentee ballots are available to be cast before candidate debates are complete.

The advocates of increased absentee balloting put forth two positive reasons in its favor. First, absentee voting is convenient. Second, the convenience of absentee balloting leads to higher voter turnout.

In Oregon, where elections are conducted by mail, surveys have shown that voters like the convenience of the system. They are happy with the system and do not want to change it. But voters also like other convenience measures that are the competitors to absentee voting. Texas, for example, has a very high percentage of voters casting their ballots before Election

Day, but at early polling places, not through the mail. And Texas voters are also happy with their convenience system. Voters do like convenience, but they like many forms of convenience.

On the question of turnout, the promise of absentee balloting leading to higher turnout has not been borne out. The assumption has been that if you remove the obstacles to voting, they will come (and vote). But extensive academic research has shown little or no positive effect from increased absentee voting or voting by mail. The one exception to these findings is that in very low turnout local elections, voting by mail does have a significant positive effect. But in statewide elections or federal elections, various studies have found a minimal effect. And to the extent that some studies have shown a small positive effect, the increase in turnout is not due to the attraction of new voters, but from a slightly higher rate of voting from those who habitually vote. The Oregon experience with all mail balloting has shown that the same voters who once went to the polls, now vote from their kitchen tables. Vote by mail has not changed who makes up the electorate, but only how they vote. Oregon election officials have often pointed to its high voter turnout as evidence of the virtues of voting by mail, but Oregon had high turnout before it instituted vote by mail.

Absentee Ballots: Where We Are and How We Got There

The first major episode of absentee balloting was during the Civil War, where soldiers in the field were able to cast ballots in the 1864 election. But after the war ended, it was not until the early part of the twentieth century that states began to introduce absentee ballots to civilians. An increasingly mobile population, traversing a vast country led states to adopt modest amounts of absentee voting for particular classes of people. States extended absentee ballots to railroad workers, government employees out of state, military voters away from home, and the sick and elderly. This revolution in voting occurred state by state, but by World War II, nearly every state had adopted some form of absentee voting.

The reformers who advocated for absentee voting saw it as a good because it extended the franchise to those who could not get to local polling places on Election Day. But these reformers also knew that absentee balloting was in conflict with another recently adopted reform, the secret ballot. In the late nineteenth century, states began to adopt the secret or "Australian ballot." These reforms consisted of a standard ballot printed by government and cast at a polling place where the voter could vote in private. The reforms were instituted to combat election fraud perpetrated by big city political machines. Before the adoption of these reforms, parties would often print up color coded ballots that voters could bring to the polls. The ballots were publicly placed in a box, so that everyone was aware if the voter had voted the proper party line. Those holding patronage jobs were expected to vote for their benefactors. Money was paid for correctly cast ballots. Punishments were meted out to renegade voters.

Within a twenty year period at the end of the 19th century, all of the states had adopted the secret ballot, and by most accounts, this reform was successful in weeding out the coercion at the polling place.

When reformers in the early twentieth century advocated for the introduction of the absentee ballot, the issue of the secret ballot was fresh in their minds. There were many legislative and state constitutional battles over whether absentee voting was constitutional, as many states had guaranteed the privacy of the vote in their constitutions. To balance the goods of privacy of the vote and offering absentee ballots to those who needed it, reformers instituted absentee ballot protections. Absentee ballots were only offered to particular classes of people who provided reasons why they needed such ballots, and procedures that preserved a degree of privacy for such ballots were instituted. The most common set of procedures was for a voter to bring his or her blank absentee ballot to a notary public, showing that the ballot had not been cast. The voter then was to fill out the ballot so that the notary public could see that no one else was filling the ballot out for them or that no one was coercing their vote. The voter would seal the ballot in an envelope, and the notary public would indicate that the ballot had been filled out properly.

States have many options to improve the convenience of elections that do not involve expanding mail or absentee ballots.

Until thirty years ago, most states had requirements like this on the books. And a few states still require witnesses or notaries in filling our absentee ballots. With this system in place, roughly five percent of voters cast their ballots by absentee. But in the 1970s, a number of states, particularly in the West, began to loosen the restrictions on casting an absentee ballot, or even actively encouraging the casting of absentee ballots. The result has been an explosion of absentee voting. Nearly 15% of Americans cast a ballot by mail in the 2004 election, and an additional 8% voted before Election Day at early polling places.

These numbers do not tell the whole story, for the rise in absentee ballots has been even more dramatic in particular states. Many northeastern, midwestern and southern states have very modest amounts of absentee voting that resembles the prevailing rate of absentee voting thirty years ago. But in the last presidential election, Oregon voted 100% by mail, Washington State almost 70%, and Arizona, California and Iowa over 30%. There are also states that have heavy early voting. Texas and Tennessee had nearly half of their voters cast votes early at polling places. Some states have a mix of both practices. Nevada, Colorado, and New Mexico had over 45% of their voters cast ballots before Election Day, either by mail or at early polling places. . . .

Advice to States on Absentee Voting

If I were testifying before a state legislature, I would urge caution in expanding absentee and vote by mail programs for many of the reasons stated above. Absentee and mail voting is convenient and liked by many voters, but it comes with a cost, especially the loss of the privacy of the ballot and additional opportunities for voter fraud. I would also note that states have many options to improve the convenience of elections that do not involve expanding mail or absentee ballots.

First, I would recommend that states significantly improve the convenience of voting on Election Day. I would recommend longer voting hours, better poll worker training, better siting of more accessible polling places. States might also consider adopting Election Day vote centers or super centers as several counties in Colorado have tried. These vote centers allow voters to cast ballots at any location in their county, not just their home polling places. Early academic research has shown that these vote centers do increase turnout and attract new voters to the process.

Second, I would recommend to states that have not already done so to explore a period of early voting at polling place locations. This would contribute to the convenience of the voting process, while retaining the protections of the polling place. Many states that have adopted early voting at polling places allow such voting two to three weeks in advance of the election. Even a week of such voting would provide significant convenience to voters, but would not substantially lengthen the period of voting. Absentee voting, on the other hand, allows for voters to cast their ballots many weeks before Election Day.

With these forms of convenience voting available to voters, there would only be a small percentage of voters who would need absentee ballots. . . .

Given the large numbers of voters casting absentee ballots, it is important for states to track and professionalize the administration of such ballots. While I am in many ways a critic of Oregon's vote by mail system, I recognize that Oregon does take the process of casting a vote by mail seriously. Unlike many states, Oregon checks a signature on each absentee ballot received. It also has an organized system for tracking ballots. . . . A simple message is: if you are going to rely heavily on absentee ballots, you need to upgrade your system of casting, tracking and counting such ballots.

Non-Citizen Voting Is a Problem

Hans A. von Spakovsky

Hans A. von Spakovsky is a former member of the Federal Election Commission and served as counsel to the Assistant Attorney General for Civil Rights at the U.S. Department of Justice.

Most people fundamentally agree with the principle that only citizens should participate in elections. Still, non-citizen voting is rampant in the United States, and debates surrounding immigration policy ignore this problem. Contrary to the assumption that undocumented immigrants wish to "stay under the radar," proof of voter registration offers them key benefits, from acquiring driver's licenses to employment eligibility. And numerous examples reveal that both illegal and legal aliens have fraudulently cast their ballots, possibly affecting tight races and the governance of the people. Thus, changes must be made at the state and federal levels to remove non-citizens from voter registration rolls and to require proper documentation to vote.

In 2005, the U.S. Government Accountability Office found that up to 3 percent of the 30,000 individuals called for jury duty from voter registration rolls over a two-year period in just one U.S. district court were not U.S. citizens. While that may not seem like many, just 3 percent of registered voters would have been more than enough to provide the winning presidential vote margin in Florida in 2000. Indeed, the Census Bureau estimates that there are over a million illegal aliens

Hans A. von Spakovsky, "Illegal Immigrants Are Voting in American Elections," *The Cutting Edge*, August 4, 2008. Reproduced by permission.

in Florida, and the U.S. Department of Justice (DOJ) has prosecuted more non-citizen voting cases in Florida than in any other state.

Florida is not unique. Thousands of non-citizens are registered to vote in some states, and tens if not hundreds of thousands in total may be present on the voter rolls nationwide. These numbers are significant: Local elections are often decided by only a handful of votes, and even national elections have likely been within the margin of the number of non-citizens illegally registered to vote.

Yet there is no reliable method to determine the number of non-citizens registered or actually voting because most laws to ensure that only citizens vote are ignored, are inadequate, or are systematically undermined by government officials. Those who ignore the implications of non-citizen registration and voting either are willfully blind to the problem or may actually favor this form of illegal voting.

Americans may disagree on many areas of immigration policy, but not on the basic principle that only citizens—and not non-citizens, whether legally present or not—should be able to vote in elections. Unless and until immigrants become citizens, they must respect the laws that bar non-citizen voting. To keep non-citizens from diluting citizens' votes, immigration and election officials must cooperate far more effectively than they have to date, and state and federal officials must increase their efforts to enforce the laws against non-citizen voting that are already on the books.

An Enduring Problem

Costas Bakouris, head of the Greek chapter of Transparency International, says in an interview that ending corruption is easy: enforce the law. Illegal voting by immigrants in America is nothing new. Almost as long as there have been elections, there have been Tammany Halls [a corrupt Democratic Party Organization] trying to game the ballot box. Well into the

20th century, the political machines asserted their ascendancy on Election Day, stealing elections in the boroughs of New York and the wards of Chicago. Quite regularly, Irish immigrants were lined up and counted in canvasses long before the term "citizen" ever applied to them—and today it is little different.

To dismiss such stolen votes because the non-citizens supposedly did not know they were acting illegally when they cast a vote debases one of the most important rights of citizens.

Yet in the debates over what to do about the 8 million to 12 million illegal aliens estimated to be in the United States, there has been virtually no discussion of how to ensure that they (and millions of legal aliens) do not register and vote in elections.

Citizenship is and should be a basic requirement for voting. Citizenship is a legal requirement to vote in federal and state elections, except for a small number of local elections in a few jurisdictions.

Some Americans argue that alien voting is a nonexistent problem or dismiss reported cases of non-citizen voting as unimportant because, they claim, there are no cases in which non-citizens "intentionally" registered to vote or voted "while knowing that they were ineligible." Even if this latter claim were true—which it is not—every vote cast by a non-citizen, whether an illegal alien or a resident alien legally in the country, dilutes or cancels the vote of a citizen and thus disenfranchises him or her. To dismiss such stolen votes because the non-citizens supposedly did not know they were acting illegally when they cast a vote debases one of the most important rights of citizens.

The evidence is indisputable that aliens, both legal and illegal, are registering and voting in federal, state, and local elections. Following a mayor's race in Compton, California, for example, aliens testified under oath in court that they voted in the election. In that case, a candidate who was elected to the city council was permanently disqualified from holding public office in California for soliciting non-citizens to register and vote. The fact that non-citizens registered and voted in the election would never have been discovered except for the fact that it was a very close election and the incumbent mayor, who lost by less than 300 votes, contested it. . . .

The "Quick Ticket"

Non-citizen voting is likely growing at the same rate as the alien population in the United States; but because of deficiencies in state law and the failure of federal agencies to comply with federal law, there are almost no procedures in place that allow election officials to detect, deter, and prevent non-citizens from registering and voting. Instead, officials are largely dependent on an "honor system" that expects aliens to follow the law. There are numerous cases showing the failure of this honor system.

The frequent claim that illegal aliens do not register in order "to stay below the radar" misses the fact that many aliens apparently believe that the potential benefit of registering far outweighs the chances of being caught and prosecuted. Many district attorneys will not prosecute what they see as a "victimless and non-violent" crime that is not a priority.

On the benefit side of the equation, a voter registration card is an easily obtainable document—they are routinely issued without any checking of identification—that an illegal alien can use for many different purposes, including obtaining a driver's license, qualifying for a job, and even voting. The Immigration Reform and Control Act of 1986, for example, requires employers to verify that all newly hired employees present documentation verifying their identity and legal authorization to work in the United States. In essence, this means that new employees have to present evidence that they are either U.S. citizens or legal aliens with a work permit. The federal I-9 form that employers must complete for all new employees provides a list of documentation that can be used to establish identity—including a voter registration card.

How aliens view the importance of this benefit was illustrated by the work of a federal grand jury in 1984 that found large numbers of aliens registered to vote in Chicago. As the grand jury reported, many aliens "register to vote so that they can obtain documents identifying them as U.S. citizens" and have "used their voters' cards to obtain a myriad of benefits, from social security to jobs with the Defense Department." The U.S. Attorney at the time estimated that there were at least 80,000 illegal aliens registered to vote in Chicago, and dozens were indicted and convicted for registering and voting.

The grand jury's report resulted in a limited cleanup of the voter registration rolls in Chicago, but just one year later, INS [Immigration and Naturalization Service] District Director A. D. Moyer testified before a state legislative task force that 25,000 illegal and 40,000 legal aliens remained on the rolls in Chicago. Moyer told the Illinois Senate that non-citizens registered so they could get a voter registration card for identification, adding that the card was "a quick ticket into the unemployment compensation system." An alien from Belize, for example, testified that he and his two sisters were able to register easily because they were not asked for any identification or proof of citizenship and lied about where they were born. After securing registration, he voted in Chicago.

Once such aliens are registered, of course, they receive the same encouragement to vote from campaigns' and parties' get-out-the-vote programs and advertisements that all other registered voters receive. Political actors have no way to distinguish between individuals who are properly registered and non-citizens who are illegally registered.

A Failure to Cooperate

Obtaining an accurate assessment of the size of this problem is difficult. There is no systematic review of voter registration rolls by states to find non-citizens, and the relevant federal agencies—in direct violation of federal law—refuse to cooperate with state election officials seeking to verify the citizenship status of registered voters. Federal immigration law requires these agencies to "respond to an inquiry by a Federal, State, or local government agency, seeking to verify or ascertain the citizenship or immigration status of any individual within the jurisdiction of the agency for any purpose authorized by law, by providing the requested verification or status information," regardless of any other provision of federal law, such as the Privacy Act. However, examples of refusal to cooperate are legion:

—In declining to cooperate with a request by Maryland to check the citizenship status of individuals registered to vote there, a spokesman for the U.S. Citizenship and Immigration Service (CIS) mistakenly declared that the agency could not release that information because "it is important to safeguard the confidentiality of each legal immigrant, especially in light of the federal Privacy Act and the Immigration and Nationality Act."

One surprising result of this policy: In 2004, a guilty verdict in a murder trial in Maryland was jeopardized because a non-citizen was discovered on the jury—which had been chosen from the voter rolls.

—In 2005, Sam Reed, the Secretary of State of Washington, asked the CIS to check the immigration status of registered voters in Washington; the agency refused to cooperate.

—A request from the Fulton County, Georgia, Board of Registration and Elections in 1998 to the old Immigration and Naturalization Service to check the immigration status of 775 registered voters was likewise refused for want of a notarized consent from each voter because of "federal privacy act" concerns. . . .

The refusal of federal agencies to obey the law compels local election officials to rely almost entirely on the "honor system" to keep non-citizens from the polls.

These incidents show that the CIS and U.S. Immigration and Customs Enforcement (ICE), the successor agencies to the INS, are either ignorant of federal legal requirements or deliberately ignoring them. An inquiry by a state or local election official regarding voter eligibility based on citizenship falls squarely within their statutory authority.

To be sure, CIS and ICE databases are not comprehensive; they contain information only about legal immigrants who have applied for the documentation necessary to be in the United States and illegal immigrants who have been detained. But even access to that information would be a big step forward for election officials in their attempts to try to clean up registration lists and find those aliens who are illegally registered and voting in elections.

The Honor System

The refusal of federal agencies to obey the law compels local election officials to rely almost entirely on the "honor system" to keep non-citizens from the polls. As Maryland's state election administrator has complained, "There is no way of checking. . . . We have no access to any information about who is in the United States legally or otherwise."

Most discoveries of non-citizens on the registration rolls are therefore accidental. Though the Department of Justice has no procedures in place for a systematic investigation of these types of criminal violations, in just a three year period, it prosecuted and convicted more than a dozen non-citizens who registered and voted in federal elections in Alaska, Florida, the District of Columbia, and Colorado. Among them was an alien in southern Florida, Rafael Velasquez, who not only voted, but even ran for the state legislature. Eight of the 19 September 11 hijackers were registered to vote in either Virginia or Florida—registrations that were probably obtained when they applied for driver's licenses.

Court clerks rarely notify local election officials that potential jurors have sworn under oath that they are not U.S. citizens.

In 1994, Mario Aburto Martinez, a Mexican national and the assassin of Mexican presidential candidate Luis Donaldo Colosio, was found to have registered twice to vote in California. A random sample of just 10 percent of the 3,000 Hispanics registered to vote in California's 39th Assembly District by an independent group "revealed phony addresses and large numbers of registrants who admitted they were not U.S. citizens." This problem may be partially explained by the testimony of a Hispanic member of the Los Angeles Police Department who had been a volunteer for the California-based Southwest Voter Registration Education Project. When she reported to her supervisor that her fellow volunteers were not asking potential voters whether they were citizens, she was reprimanded "and told that she was not to ask that question . . . only whether the person wished to register to vote." . . .

Some non-citizen registrations can be detected through the jury process. The vast majority of state and federal courts draw their jury pools from voter registration lists, and the jury questionnaires used by court clerks ask potential jurors whether they are U.S. citizens. In most states, however, and throughout the federal court system, court clerks rarely notify local election officials that potential jurors have sworn under oath that they are not U.S. citizens. In jurisdictions that share that information, election officials routinely discover non-citizens on the voter rolls. For example, the district attorney in Maricopa County, Arizona, testified that after receiving a list of potential jurors who admitted they were not citizens, he indicted 10 who had registered to vote. (All had sworn on their registration forms that they were U.S. citizens.) Four had actually voted in elections. The district attorney was investigating 149 other cases. . . .

Helping Aliens Vote

Under the Constitution, an individual's eligibility to vote is left mostly to the states. Article I and the 17th Amendment provide that the electors for Members of Congress shall have the qualifications for electors of the most numerous branch of the state legislatures. Article II provides that presidential electors shall be chosen in the manner directed by state legislatures. All of the states require voters to be U.S. citizens to vote in state elections, and 18 U.S.C. § 611 makes it a crime for "any alien to vote in any election held solely or in part for the purpose of electing a candidate for the office of President, Vice President, Presidential elector," or Congress.

Other federal laws authorize the Justice Department to prosecute non-citizens for registering and voting in elections. The National Voter Registration Act of 1993 (NVRA) requires individuals registering to vote to affirm eligibility requirements, including citizenship. The Help America Vote Act of 2002 (HAVA) added a specific citizenship question to the federal voter registration form. Since citizenship is clearly material to a voter's eligibility, aliens can be prosecuted for providing false registration information and voting under the NVRA. They can also be prosecuted under 18 U.S.C. § 1015(f), which criminalizes making a false statement or claim about citizenship "in order to register to vote or to vote in any Federal, State, or local election (including an initiative, recall, or referendum)," and under 18 U.S.C. § 911, which prohibits making a false claim of citizenship.

The NVRA has contributed to the problem of aliens registering to vote. The largest source of voter registrations is state programs created under Section 5 of the NVRA, known as "Motor Voter," which requires all states to allow individuals who apply for a driver's license to register to vote at the same time. States such as Maryland, Hawaii, Maine, Michigan, New Mexico, Oregon, Utah, and Washington allow illegal aliens to obtain driver's licenses, and other states, such as Tennessee, provide licenses to resident aliens.

To comply with Motor Voter, states automatically offer voter registration to all applicants for a driver's license. Most government employees do so even when they know the applicants are not citizens because these employees do not want to face claims that they discriminated based on ethnicity, and they believe it is the responsibility of election officials, not state DMVs [Department of Motor Vehicles], to determine the eligibility of voter registration applicants. Yet when license bureaus submit completed registration forms to state election officials, they often omit the citizenship status of the applicants.

All states should require anyone who registers to vote to provide proof of U.S. citizenship.

Savvy politicians may already have taken advantage of this state of affairs. During the Clinton Administration, for example, the Justice Department allegedly forced states to offer voter registration to non-citizens. In response, the Texas Secretary of State reportedly asked his attorney general to sue the department. . . .

Practical Solutions

There are several changes that states and the federal government can and should make to prevent non-citizens from registering and voting illegally in state and federal elections:

—Congress and state legislatures should require all federal and state courts to notify local election officials when individuals summoned for jury duty from voter registration rolls are excused because they are not United States citizens. United States Attorneys are already under a similar obligation: Under the NVRA, they must send information on felony convictions to local election officials so that the felons can be removed from voter registration rolls.

—All states should require anyone who registers to vote to provide proof of U.S. citizenship. This requirement should be identical to the federal requirement of proof for employment.

—ICE and CIS should comply with federal law and confirm the citizenship status of registered voters when they receive requests for such information from state and local election officials. If the agencies decline to do so, they should be investigated by Congress and the Inspector General of the Department of Homeland Security (DHS) for their failure to follow the law. . . .

America has always been a nation of immigrants, and we remain today the most welcoming nation in the world. Newly minted citizens assimilate and become part of the American culture very quickly. Requiring that our laws—all of our laws—be complied with requires no more of an alien than it does of a citizen. It is a violation of both state and federal law for immigrants who are not citizens to vote in state and federal elections. These violations effectively disenfranchise legitimate voters whose votes are diluted, and they must be curtailed.

Election officials have an obligation not only to enforce those laws, but also to implement registration and election procedures that do not allow those laws to be bypassed or ignored. Anything less encourages contempt for the law and our election process. Lax enforcement of election laws permits individuals who have not entered the American social compact or made a commitment to the U.S. Constitution, U.S. laws, and the U.S. cultural and political heritage to participate in elections and potentially change the outcome of closely contested races that affect how all Americans are governed.

Non-Citizen and Voter Identification Laws Are Discriminatory

Garrett Epps

Garrett Epps is a law professor at the University of Baltimore and author of Democracy Reborn: The Fourteenth Amendment and the Fight for Equal Rights in Post-Civil War America.

A continuum of voter identification laws in the United States is supposedly designed to deter non-citizen and unregistered voters from fraud. But the widespread "voter impersonations" purported by conservatives, the main backers of such restrictions, are all but unknown in the country today. In fact, identification laws single out the poor, the elderly, and ethnic groups (who are less likely to have certain forms of documentation)—and it is not by chance that these targeted groups tend to vote for liberals. Clearly, voter suppression continues in contemporary America. It is mortifying that the right to vote is not guaranteed to every eligible, competent citizen, and that marginalized voters remain under intimidation.

There's a war on across the country over who will be allowed to vote in 2008. One of the key battles in the election was fought on January 9 before the Supreme Court.

The case is called *Crawford v. Marion County Election Board*. It tests an Indiana statute, passed in 2005, requiring voters to present a government-issued ID before they can cast

Garrett Epps, "The Voter ID Fraud," *Nation*, January 10, 2008. Reproduced by permission.

a ballot. The law is aimed at alleged fraudulent voting by un-registered or noncitizen voters. Republicans insist that these voters pose a major problem, despite the fact that every systematic study of the question has concluded that this kind of fraud—called "voter impersonation"—is all but unknown in the United States right now. In fact, authorities in Indiana could not point to a single case of voter impersonation in the state's history.

Voter ID laws span a wide spectrum. The federal Help America Vote Act (HAVA), passed in 2002, provides that all states must require ID from first-time voters who register by mail. But twenty-five states and the District of Columbia have gone beyond this. Eighteen require all voters to produce some form of ID, which may be a bank statement or utility bill sent to their address. Two require a photo ID, which may include employee or other unofficial IDs. Arizona requires all voters to produce either one government-issued ID or two other identifications. Indiana stands alone in requiring that the ID have a photo and be issued by the government—the most difficult forms of identification to obtain. Voters who don't have such IDs are supposed to cast "provisional" ballots, which will be counted only if they show up at election headquarters with a proper ID within a few days of the voting.

The more restrictive the law, the greater the likelihood that it will tip a close election by turning away legal voters—mostly the poor, minorities and the elderly. It's not a coincidence that these voters tend to vote Democratic. In fact, the State of Indiana, in its filings with the Supreme Court, admits that the litigation represents "politics by other means." This flippant attitude toward the right to vote permeates the state's argument. Unfortunately, the Supreme Court has shown signs that it shares the view that turning voters away from the polls is constitutionally unimportant.

A coalition of Democratic Party officials and activists promptly challenged the Indiana law. A federal district court dismissed their challenge on the ground that they had not shown that the law would actually prevent anyone from voting. The plaintiffs presented an exhaustive study by a well-known election expert estimating the number of registered Indiana voters who lacked ID at nearly 1 million; the district judge, however, dismissed the report as "utterly incredible and unreliable."

On appeal, Judge Richard Posner of the Seventh Circuit admitted that "some people who have not bothered to obtain a photo ID will not bother to do so just to be allowed to vote." He further admits that "no doubt most people who don't have photo ID are low on the economic ladder and thus, if they do vote, are more likely to vote for Democratic than Republican candidates." But what's the big deal? It's only a few voters.

So what if there's no evidence of voter impersonation? That's the media's fault, Posner says. The lack of cases "may reflect nothing more than the vagaries of journalists' and other investigators' choice of scandals to investigate."

Even without the ID law, voters in Indiana and elsewhere often must show evidence of eligibility. In some states the voter must sign a polling book before receiving a ballot. Election officials compare the signature with an official one on file. In addition, poll watchers from the two parties can look at the book and challenge any voter whose signature doesn't appear to match. Partisan poll watchers have every incentive to check the signatures carefully.

In recent years, conservative groups have insisted that precedence should go to "legitimate" voters, the kind of people who have ready access to ID.

No one on either side of the issue disputes that voter fraud occurs. But study after study has made clear that documented fraud is almost exclusively confined to absentee ballots. Absentee voting is one area where Republicans have tra-ditionally out-organized Democrats; the new voter ID laws make almost no reforms to the absentee-vote system.

A Duel over Common Sense

The voter-fraud argument comes down to a kind of duel over common sense. Voter ID proponents dismiss the lack of evidence; it stands to reason, they say, that if requirements are not strict, ineligible people will vote. Opponents counter that if it's hard to vote, some legal voters won't go to the polls. Whose votes matter? In recent years, conservative groups have insisted that precedence should go to "legitimate" voters, the kind of people who have ready access to ID. After all, Posner notes, "try flying, or even entering a tall building such as the courthouse in which we sit, without one." The roughly 18 percent of Americans who have never flown on a commercial airline are less worthy of concern.

The Indiana case will likely have an influence on a number of ID cases around the country. Arizona has in place a law requiring voters to prove their citizenship by presenting not just a driver's license but a passport or birth certificate upon registering and a photo ID at the polls. The city of Albuquerque changed its charter to require a photo ID at the polls. In Georgia the Republican legislature voted to require government-issued ID; the same session of the legislature voted to double the fee for such an ID. A federal court in Georgia initially blocked that ID law but then dismissed the challenge after the legislature amended the statute to waive the fee. The Albuquerque charter amendment has been stayed by a federal judge; the Georgia case is on appeal. At stake is the potential margin of victory in a close election.

If you doubt that, consider Missouri. Its law—the most restrictive in the country—was struck down before the 2006 election as a violation of the state Constitution. Senator Claire

McCaskill went on to defeat Republican incumbent Jim Talent by a mere 48,314 votes out of 2,128,455 cast, a margin of only 2.3 percent.

The strongest argument *for* ID laws arises from the 1993 National Voter Registration Act, also known as the "motor voter" law. This act encourages mail-in voter registration and mandates that the states distribute registration forms at their driver's license bureaus. The result has been an increase in duplicate or obsolete registrations on state voter rolls, which could lead to mischief. The Help America Vote Act requires states to centralize voter lists and eliminate duplicate registrations. But many states haven't done so. Nevertheless, inflated voter rolls are a separate problem, which can be addressed by funding and implementing HAVA. To justify ID requirements, advocates need to provide evidence of voter fraud.

In the turn-of-the-century South, voter restriction was a keystone of the burgeoning segregated system.

The obsession with voter fraud has been orchestrated by the Republican Party, with [former White House Deputy Chief of staff] Karl Rove playing a significant role. The US Attorney firings scandal under Alberto Gonzales seems to have stemmed, in part, from Republicans' desire to push federal prosecutors into going after voters' rights and poor people's groups like ACORN [Association of Community Organizers for Reform Now] for their turn-out-the-vote activities. In Wisconsin, voter fraud prosecutions netted convictions of a number of small-fish activists who mishandled registration cards and individual voters who filled out two registration cards or attempted to vote despite being convicted felons or on criminal probation. Prosecutors have lost more than half the cases they've brought. In Washington, where Democrat Christine Gregoire narrowly defeated Dino Rossi for governor in 2004, officials of the Justice Department removed US Attorney John McKay, who refused to bring voter fraud charges tied to the election.

Lacking evidence, the Republicans have shifted their argument. Now it runs: "legitimate voters" will lose confidence in elections if they think there's voter fraud, so the government must clamp down even without evidence. Unfortunately, there are signs that the Supreme Court has bought this New Age-y "voter feelings" argument. In early 2006, voters' rights groups challenged the Arizona law requiring proof of citizenship. The Ninth Circuit enjoined the law pending a full trial; the state appealed to the US Supreme Court, which allowed the law to take effect without a trial. Some voters "who fear their legitimate votes will be outweighed by fraudulent ones will feel disenfranchised," the Court reasoned in an unsigned opinion. The case is awaiting a full trial. A study has shown that some 5,000 voter registrations in Arizona, virtually all for eligible voters, were rejected in a six-month period for failure to provide proof of citizenship.

Folklore and the History of Voter Fraud

Folklore pervades the history of voter fraud in the United States. During the era of "live voice" voting, when voters shouted their choices in front of their neighbors, there was rampant bribery, intimidation, miscounting and voter impersonation. Roving gangs of ringers, plied with whiskey and $2 bills, voted in multiple locations under false names.

During the Gilded Age and the Progressive era, as Alex Keyssar documents in his monumental study *The Right to Vote: The Contested History of Democracy in the United States*, the idea of the fraudulent voter coincided with social anxiety among the "better sort" about the political influence of the uneducated and recent immigrants. Whether or not they were legally entitled to vote, their votes were seen almost as fraudulent per se. In the turn-of-the-century South, voter restriction was a keystone of the burgeoning segregated system. "Voter fraud" meant votes cast by black and poor white voters. In the West, fraud meant voting by Native Americans.

The current restriction movement preys on a new wave of immigration anxiety. In his 2004 book *Stealing Elections*, John Fund, now an editorialist for the *Wall Street Journal*, warned dramatically that "at least eight of the nineteen hijackers who attacked the World Trade Center and the Pentagon were actually able to register to vote in either Virginia or Florida while they made their deadly preparations for 9/11." (Fund told me that the information came from an interview with Michael Chertoff, now Secretary of Homeland Security, while he was a Justice Department official. Fund suggested that Chertoff's statement may have come from secret information. Two academics—Spencer Overton of George Washington University and Lorraine Minnite of Barnard—have been unable to confirm the "registered hijacker" claim with election officials.)

The issue in *Crawford v. Marion County Election Board* is likely to boil down to a complex legal concept that lawyers call the "level of scrutiny." This refers to the degree of proof that courts require to justify a government action. If a law restricts a trivial right, such as the right to smoke in public, all they need is a decent reason; if it restricts a fundamental right, like the right to travel interstate, officials must offer a convincing explanation and actual facts to support the law.

So the question will be: is making it burdensome or impossible for some people to vote a trivial abridgment or a serious impairment of an important part of full citizenship? Posner's opinion makes clear his view that casting an individual vote is no big deal. He cites a 1992 Supreme Court case, *Burdick v. Takushi*, that upheld a Hawaii ban on write-in voting. In *Burdick*, the Court said that strict scrutiny applied only to "severe" burdens of the individual's right to participate in elections. Regulations that, for example, limit the choice of candidates, however, need only be "reasonable" and "nondiscriminatory." (Interestingly, Justice Anthony Kennedy, whose vote is always decisive in close cases, dissented in *Burdick*, holding that the Hawaii write-in ban did not pass even loose scrutiny.)

But *Burdick* concerned the voters' right to choose a candidate not on the ballot—the Hawaii law did not deprive anyone of the right to cast a vote. Earlier cases have suggested that measures barring voters altogether are subject to "strict scrutiny," the standard that applies to proving government discrimination by race. If strict scrutiny is in effect, then officials in Indiana and elsewhere would actually have to produce facts to support their statute. It would certainly be impossible to be as flippant as Posner was about the flaws in the Indiana statute: "Perhaps the Indiana law can be improved—what can't be?"

In virtually every other advanced democracy, voting has a positive value: it is not up to the citizen to seek out a registrar or produce a satisfactory ID.

The subtext of this case, and of the war over the vote, is a defect in America's patchwork Constitution. Unlike virtually every modern democratic constitution, ours nowhere explicitly guarantees every competent citizen the right to vote. States can't restrict the vote by race, or sex, or failure to pay a poll tax, or by age for anyone over 18; but the document nowhere says that eligible voters have a right to their vote. In fact, when Supreme Court Justices discuss voting rights, they often refer to this most basic of rights in scare quotes—"the 'right' to vote." This allows judges to adopt a kind of faux neutrality: some people want to vote; others don't want them to vote— the outcome is merely a matter of expediency.

This is desperately wrongheaded. In virtually every other advanced democracy, voting has a positive value: it is not up to the citizen to seek out a registrar or produce a satisfactory

ID. Instead, the government itself is required to find and register every eligible voter and, if necessary, to provide each voter with an official ID without charge.

Amending the Constitution to guarantee the vote is an important long-term goal. But Congress can do much to ensure that this mischief does not grow, spread and become entrenched. Article I, Section 4, declares that the states shall regulate elections, unless Congress steps in. Congress could pass a statute requiring states to conduct fair, nonpartisan registration and to allow citizens to vote with a signature.

A Mortal Flaw in the System

Currently before Congress are a variety of piecemeal reforms. Hillary Clinton's wide-ranging Count Every Vote bill would require states to accept an affidavit of citizenship as part of the mail-in registration process and would make it harder for state officials to toss out mail-in registrations for small errors. Barack Obama has a narrower bill aimed at measures that deceive voters about their eligibility. Representative Keith Ellison has offered legislation to block state ID requirements, but his bill has sparked little support.

The ID issue should be higher on the Democratic agenda. Voting is more than a matter of individual preference, like Coke or Pepsi. Free participation protects our political system from a more insidious kind of corruption in which elites govern without undue worry about public repudiation.

Vote suppression in the United States has a long and sordid past and present. Anonymous postcards often warn registered voters in black neighborhoods that they are ineligible. Fliers warn that any voter with an outstanding warrant will be arrested at the polls. Phone calls threaten eligible voters with criminal prosecution.

Thirty years ago, I saw white Southern registrars driving black voters away by threatening them with federal voter fraud charges. In 2004 I received an e-mail from my son, from a

Southern election headquarters. He was fielding calls from black voters who were being turned away from the polls for minor errors in registration or failure to show an ID.

It is mortifying that we are passing this mortal flaw in our system down to the next generation. Voting lies at the heart of our national life, and efforts to restrict it to the "right" people corrode our very commitment to freedom. Perhaps we should consider radical change in our system.

Perhaps we should consider democracy.

9

Counting the Votes of Deceased Voters Is a Problem

Marcel Dufresne

Marcel Dufresne is a journalism professor at the University of Connecticut.

An investigation by University of Connecticut journalism students reveals that ballots from deceased state residents have been cast and counted years after their deaths. In addition, more than 8,500 dead people were still registered to vote. The investigation yielded no evidence of intentional fraud, but it highlights the risk of clerical error and potential for abuse of Connecticut's voter database. Similar names of deceased and living persons caused some confusion, and, in other cases, death certificates were not forwarded to the proper offices. The computerization and consolidation of state databases and records offer possible solutions, but such projects are currently works in progress.

Jane M. Drury, homemaker, mother, grandmother and great-grandmother, spent most of her life in Staten Island, N.Y., but moved to Stonington [Connecticut] in 1992 to live with her daughter. That October, she registered to vote there.

State records show Drury never actually voted in Stonington before her death in 2000 in a Groton nursing home at age 97. But the same records say she did vote in Stonington once since then—in a 2007 budget referendum.

That recorded vote, seven years after her death, puts Drury on a list of more than 300 people across Connecticut who ap-

Marcel Dufresne, "Dead Voters? Probe Finds Errors in Records," *Hartford Courant*, April 20, 2008. Reproduced by permission of *Los Angeles Times*.

pear to have voted from the grave in elections dating to 1994, a two-month investigation of voting records by journalism students at the University of Connecticut [UConn] has found.

The mysterious voters were identified by matching a statewide database of 2 million registered voters and their voting histories with two separate computer lists of dead people maintained by the state Department of Public Health and the federal Social Security Administration.

Following up on the matches, UConn students examined the records of nearly 100 of the suspect voters at 10 town and city halls among those with the most cases. Guilford led the state with 39, followed by West Hartford (17), Enfield (15), Stonington (13) and Norwalk (11).

Some people appeared to have voted frequently after death, the research found. In Hebron, for example, records show one man voted 17 times after he died in 1992.

The findings reveal flaws in the voting system and expose its vulnerability to potential abuse.

The investigation also identified more than 8,500 people listed as dead who are still registered to vote in Connecticut, most long after their deaths. In Hamden, one woman remained a registered voter although she died in 1979.

Although the investigation found no evidence of deliberate fraud, it uncovered numerous errors in voting and registration records kept by local registrars, and highlights weaknesses in a state voter database established in the mid-1990s, ostensibly to prevent fraud and duplicate voting.

State elections officials and others concede that the findings reveal flaws in the voting system and expose its vulnerability to potential abuse.

"I understood [dead voters] as a myth," said Joan M. Andrews, enforcement director for the State Elections Enforcement Commission, which investigates elections and campaign finance irregularities. "People make jokes about dead people voting but we never thought things like that could actually happen."

Andrews said she plans to bring the UConn findings to the full commission to determine whether further investigation is warranted.

Trouble in Town Hall

Michael Kozik, managing attorney for the secretary of the state's office, which is responsible for the state database, said he was most troubled by the thousands of dead people still registered to vote. "Clearly this is an issue that we need to look at," he said.

All but nine of Connecticut's 169 municipalities listed dead people on active voter rolls. At least 100 cases were identified in each of 28 cities and towns. In New Haven alone, 370 dead people were still registered; in Enfield there were 321; in West Haven, 310; in Hartford, 298; and in Bridgeport, 293.

The UConn investigation also found instances of people who were not registered yet were able to vote—under a dead person's name—along with frequent discrepancies between the state data and paper voting records at local town halls.

The potential for fraud is most serious in municipal elections, when officials are not required to check photo identification at the polls and voters need only sign a statement attesting to their identity.

The UConn findings highlight two nagging problems facing officials trying to keep accurate voting records. First is the informal and antiquated ways many local registrars remove dead people from voter rolls. Second is the potential for clerical errors when registrars transfer information from paper voting lists to the state database, especially in the rush to update by the two-day, post-election deadline.

Many of those interviewed blame a locally based election system that has not changed much in decades. In many towns, elections and voter registration are run by part-time registrars who are paid little, have limited resources, and may resist the growing role of computers in elections.

By all official records, [Jane M.] Drury voted seven years after she had died.

The UConn findings are disturbing but not surprising, said Andy Sauer, executive director of Connecticut Common Cause, a public-interest group that lobbies for election reform. He blamed many of the system's problems on politically appointed local registrars using outdated methods of running elections and keeping records. Each town has two registrars, one Democrat and one Republican.

"You need to take the election administration out of the hands of a politician and into the hands of a state administration," he said, a solution many in the system might consider unrealistic.

Figuring out Who Died

Jane Drury's vote in a May 2007 Stonington referendum, first detected in the state data, was later confirmed on a paper check-off list at the town hall showing her name crossed off with a straight line. By all official records, Drury voted seven years after she had died.

"Somebody goofed, obviously," said Jane Gumpel, Drury's daughter. "I don't know how that could happen."

Louise Brown, a Stonington registrar of voters, was one of several municipal registrars who initially expressed skepticism when informed that dead people appeared to be voting in their town. Brown was shown a list of 13 dead people who state records indicated had voted a total of 38 times in Stonington since 2001. A quick check of several names confirmed the problems, and Brown began tracking down several suspicious cases. Registrars in other towns responded similarly.

Around the state, UConn students identified a variety of explanations for why people seemed to be voting after death. The most common was clerical errors made while checking off voters' names at the polls or entering votes into the state database.

In other cases, someone with the same name, sometimes a relative who was not registered, actually cast the vote. Other times, a living person might have been mistakenly taken off the rolls when someone with the same name died. Votes in both scenarios were erroneously credited to a dead person.

Connecticut is one of many states with no formal system for notifying registrars when someone dies. Death certificates are sent to the city or town where the death occurs, not necessarily where people lived, even if they lived in the same town all their lives. When someone dies in a hospital or nursing home in another town or an adjacent state, the death certificate may never come to the registrars' attention.

Registrars tend to rely on newspaper obituaries, relatives, or word of mouth to learn of someone's death, many officials said.

Even then, registrars are advised to be extremely cautious about purging dead people from voter rolls, said George Cody, president of the Registrar of Voters Association of Connecticut and New Canaan's Democratic registrar. They must see documentary proof, such as the death certificate or a published obituary, before removing someone's name.

A Confusion of Names

The possibility that two or more people in the same town have the same name makes registrars especially cautious about removing a voter, Cody said.

Identical names seem to explain the case of George E. Gagnon, a retired auto body repairman who, records indicate, voted seven times in East Hartford after his death on June 15,

1991, with all of the votes coming after 2001. Gagnon, born in 1918, had moved to neighboring Manchester in 1952, long before he died.

It turns out that a different George E. Gagnon, a retired truck driver born in 1921, is very much alive, living and voting regularly in East Hartford.

While registrars are reluctant to cancel a voter's registration without physical proof of death, they are under no obligation to seek out such proof.

"A lot of dead people vote in this state," the living Gagnon joked after finding out a different George Gagnon had been credited with his votes. "I'm still alive and if somebody makes a mistake, that's not my fault."

The explanation: Someone at the East Hartford registrars office entered the living Gagnon into the state database using the birth date on the other Gagnon's registration card, even though the latter had left town 50 years earlier. As a result, the living Gagnon was identified as dead in the computer match and the dead Gagnon appeared to have cast multiple votes in East Hartford.

While registrars are reluctant to cancel a voter's registration without physical proof of death, they are under no obligation to seek out such proof, even when it might be filed elsewhere in their own town hall. UConn students found numerous cases in which death and burial certificates on file in one town office did not find their way to registrars in the same building.

State records show that Carmella Vella, an Italian immigrant who settled in Enfield in 1913, voted there in 2005 and 2006. But Vella died across the state border in a Springfield hospital in 1998. The votes, it turned out, stem from clerical errors.

Neighboring towns are supposed to forward death certificates to a dead person's hometown, but that doesn't always happen, said Enfield's recently retired Republican registrar, Vaughan Vanderscoff.

But proof of Vella's death—a burial certificate for an Enfield cemetery—is on file in the town clerk's office down the hall from the registrar.

Vella's daughter-in-law, Barbara Vella, said she doesn't understand why her husband's mother was still registered.

"I've told them multiple times to take her off the list," Vella said. "She is certainly deceased."

Kozik, of the secretary of the state's office, concedes: "There should be a better system of getting the death information to the registrars in a timely fashion. But I'm not exactly sure how we would do that."

How Mistakes Are Made

In theory, at least, there is a simple way to supply registrars with accurate death information. The state Office of Vital Records maintains a database of death certificates in Connecticut—called the "consolidated master death file"—dating to 1949. It is the same database used by UConn students to identify votes attributed to dead people.

A 2005 report to Congress by the Government Accountability Office [GAO] recommended that states share computerized death certificate data with towns to accurately purge dead people from voter rolls. Georgia began doing so in 2003, after a newspaper investigation revealed some 15,000 dead people still registered in that state.

But Kozik, who was not familiar with the GAO recommendation, cautioned against using computer matching alone to remove voters' names.

"I would always be reluctant to have computers automatically disenfranchising people to vote," Kozik said. "Before someone is actually taken off the list I would want some kind of human intervention and judgment involved."

Many votes credited to dead people appeared to result from clerical error, UConn students found.

In Southington, the state data show that 10 dead people voted, most in November 2000. But a check of paper records showed none actually had voted.

Checkers at the polls mistakenly cross off sons instead of fathers, and vice versa, or cross off neighbors who have similar names.

"The errors had to occur when we were typing the names of people who voted into the computer," said Carol Sheffs, deputy registrar in Southington. "Everyone is in a rush to see who voted. You do it fast and you don't have time to check over your work. That's how mistakes are made."

Local officials are well aware of the system's weaknesses, said Carole Young-Kleinfeld, a deputy registrar in Wilton and a spokeswoman for the Connecticut League of Women Voters. "The possibility of human error at election time is very real. Checkers at the polls mistakenly cross off sons instead of fathers, and vice versa, or cross off neighbors who have similar names."

Kozik downplayed the significance of voter history errors. Those records are kept mostly as a convenience to political parties, which use the information to target frequent voters, he said.

But Andrews, of the elections enforcement commission, said a state record that shows who voted and who did not should be accurate. Especially troubling, she said, are those dead people whose votes are confirmed by check-off lists, which can only result from multiple errors in the process.

She described most problems as "systematic" and blamed them on "a lack of uniformity" at the local level. Municipali-

ties are supposed to follow the same state-mandated procedures, she said, "but when you go out to a town, you find that
they aren't."

Forced to Go Online

UConn students found 10 cases in which an unregistered person was able to vote under a dead person's name. In most
cases, the person was a son or daughter with the same first,
last and middle name, and sometimes even the same address,
but not the same date of birth.

One such case involved Donald R. Tichy Jr., a 1981 gradu-
ate of the University of Hartford, who died of cancer in 1992
at the age of 33. Votes attributed to Tichy in 2005 and 2006
were actually cast by his father, Donald R. Tichy Sr. The only
registration card under the name of Donald Tichy lists the
son's identification information, plus the suffix "Jr." added, in
pencil, after the name.

"I've been voting illegally, is what you're telling me," a surprised Tichy Sr. said. He vowed to straighten out the matter.

The secretary of the state's office created the voter database in the mid-1990s to help detect fraud and duplicate registrations, years ahead of the 2002 federal Help America Vote
Act that required every state to keep such a database.

Participation by local registrars was voluntary at first—
some towns resisted the move to computerization—but the
state legislature required every town to go online by September 2003.

Calling the database "a work in progress," Andrews noted
that some towns had to be forced to comply. In Norwalk, two
registrars were fined $1,500 each for failing to complete their
portion of the registry on time and for not using it in the November 2004 election.

State officials say they have known of problems with the
database since 2005, when the elections enforcement commis-

sion tested the system, looking for people who might have voted twice in the 2004 national election, Andrews said.

The agency initially was surprised to find more than 400 people who apparently voted more than once. But after spending more than a year investigating each case, the agency found no evidence of duplicate voting.

"One by one, there turned out to be some sort of explanation for them." Andrews said. The investigation found many of the same causes identified in the UConn investigation.

Some officials suggest that better training for registrars would improve the system. The secretary of the state's office and the registrars association have been conducting "a very intensive training program" for registrars for nearly two years, especially those newly elected, said Cody, the registrars association president.

But he conceded that some registrars, especially those in smaller towns, whom he described as "woefully underpaid and understaffed," may be slow to adapt.

"We can lead them to water," Cody said, "but we can't make them drink."

10

Counting the Votes of Deceased Voters Is Not a Problem

Justin Levitt

Justin Levitt is an associate counsel at the Brennan Center for Justice at the New York University School of Law. He focuses on voting-rights issues, such as redistricting and election administration.

News stories about hordes of voters coming back from the dead and casting their ballots are misleading, unreliable, and predictable. Registration rolls are exhumed and potential matches are flagged, resulting in routine undead voter headlines. But the real culprit is mundane—erroneous list matches often result in mixups between the dead and living, and a major list, the Social Security Administration's "Death Master File," is woefully inaccurate. What's really scary? The manipulation of the dead voter hoax to justify voter identification laws, which are extraneous and unduly burden the electorate.

Once again, it's late October [2006], the time of year when wholesome communities across America enjoy some good-natured fictional fearmongering. Ghostly apparitions are everywhere, and everyone's chuckling. Of course, this is also election season—and for the press, the connection is often irresistible. The dearly departed . . . are alive and voting. Boo!

Dead-voter pieces appear as reliably as slasher-movie sequels, and are about as straightforward to write. Registration

Justin Levitt, "Raising the Dead Voter Hoax," TompPaine.com, October 31, 2006. Reproduced by permission.

rolls are mined for entries of the recently and not-so-recently deceased. A list of ostensible voters and a list of ostensible corpses are run through a computer program that spits out potential matches. Many thousands of entries are flagged. And voila: The horde of allegedly undead voters makes the front page.

These undead voters, however, don't do well in daylight. Problems with matching from list to list often account for much of the alleged fraud. For example, statistics tell us that two individuals share the same name, even the same birthdate, with surprising frequency, so that two people—one dead, one very much alive—may be confused for each other.

There are additional problems with the underlying lists themselves. The Social Security Administration's "Death Master File"—the most common source for seeking fraud—is notoriously inaccurate when used in this manner, listing as deceased hundreds of thousands of citizens who are in the best of health. And pollworkers make mistakes, checking a box one entry down or one entry up from the correct line, so that the wrong individual appears to have voted.

These problems can usually be overcome, but only with substantial effort. Sophisticated computer algorithms may be able to match list to list more reliably, but are usually proprietary and often expensive. Phone calls to speak with the families of flagged voters are both awkward and time-consuming. And even if the actual poll records have not been discarded, going to the original source to check for recordkeeping errors is a bureaucratic pain in the neck.

As a result, reliable reporting on dead-voter stories is frighteningly rare.

Unwarranted Headlines

A story this past Sunday [October 2006] from upstate New York provides an intriguing example of the best—and worst—of the coverage. The usual lists were matched. The usual caveats were proffered. But then the intrepid reporter went beyond the superficial. He acknowledged—twice!—that most instances of dead voters "can be attributed to database mismatches and clerical errors." He presented an actual citizen who was listed as dead but was in fact breathing soundly. He found an absentee ballot that had incorrectly been attributed to a deceased family member of the actual voter.

And yet, the unwarranted headline: "Dead voters continue to cast ballots in New York."

Boo!

When the deceased show up in unfounded reports of election fraud, it's not just good holiday entertainment. Indeed, a recent status report on an investigation of voter fraud under the auspices of the bipartisan federal Election Assistance Commission noted the large number of unsupported fraud claims in recent stories, and cited allegations that the unfounded charges were "an effort to scare people away from the voting process."

For the moment, the Commission has—ahem—buried the full results of the investigation itself, which should catalog both the allegations and the inaccuracies, if not the motivation behind the stories. But whether or not the false charges are actually intended to frighten, the repeated cries of "wolf" lead Americans to lose trust in a part of the election process that actually works fairly well, and distracts them from fixing the parts of the process that need substantial overhaul.

This, in turn, leads to policies that truly deserve scary headlines.

For example, consider the recent voter-ID legislation passed by the U.S. House of Representatives and justified in substantial part by dead-voter stories. Never mind that federal law already puts the burden on states to clean deceased registrants from new statewide voter registration lists, carefully and with safeguards for legitimate voters. This new bill would instead confront the illusory dead-voter problem by placing a new burden on the electorate: all citizens would be required to show government-issued documentary identification with a photo and proof of citizenship before voting.

Let's leave the undead voter hordes to the fiction section, where they belong.

It is appropriate that the bill was first sponsored by Representative [Henry] Hyde—a name with substantial Halloween resonance—because it would have some truly ghoulish effects. At the moment, only a passport or a driver's license from one of three states would satisfy Hyde's standards. Any voter without the magic documents—even those citizens legitimately voting for years or decades—would suddenly find the doors of the polling place mysteriously shut.

The usual claim is that laws like these are justified, despite their profoundly disenfranchising effect, to ward off the forces of fraud. Dead voters, in particular, provide powerful anecdotal evidence that these sorts of rules are necessary. Which is why it is so dangerous to repeat dead-voter anecdotes that later prove untrue. Even if—especially if—it's only in a headline.

We would all be better served by a little more restraint. Yes, as states continue to clean new registration rolls, there will still be a dwindling number of deceased registrants who remain on the list. But on Election Day, they generally rest in peace.

This Halloween, there are more than enough scary stories of verified wrongs to fill the newspaper pages. Let's leave the undead voter hordes to the fiction section, where they belong.

Organizations to Contact

The editors have compiled the following list of organizations concerned with the issues debated in this book. The descriptions are derived from materials provided by the organizations. All have publications or information available for interested readers. The list was compiled on the date of publication of the present volume; the information provided here may change. Readers need to remember that many organizations take several weeks or longer to respond to inquiries.

American Civil Liberties Union (ACLU)
125 Broad St., 18th Fl., New York, NY 10004
Web site: www.aclu.org

Founded in 1920, the ACLU is a nonprofit and nonpartisan organization that focuses on basic freedoms. It has more than 500,000 members and supporters and handles nearly 6,000 court cases annually from its offices in almost every state. The ACLU addresses issues such as voter fraud and it challenges voter identification laws, both of which are topics of commentary on the organization's Web site.

Association of Community Organizations for Reform Now (ACORN)
2609 Canal St., New Orleans, LA 70119
(504) 943-0044
Web site: www.acorn.org

ACORN is the nation's largest grassroots community organization of low- and moderate-income people with more than 400,000 member families organized into more than 1,200 neighborhood chapters in 110 cities across the country. ACORN members and workers go door-to-door in low- and moderate-income neighborhoods; approach people at shopping centers, grocery stores, and libraries; and visit high schools to talk to voting-age students in an effort to encourage as many people as possible to participate in the democratic process. ACORN publishes reports regarding voting legislation and a monthly e-newsletter.

Center for Voter Advocacy (CVA)

PO Box 9601, Coral Springs, FL   33075
(954) 692-3486
e-mail: info@centerforvoteradvocacy.org
Web site: www.centerforvoteradvocacy.org

The CVA seeks to promote the values of democracy and political efficacy within local communities, educate Americans about the political process to effectively make a positive difference, and serve as a vehicle for political expression. The nonprofit organization sponsors various events and activities that promote civic engagement.

Committee to Modernize Voter Registration

e-mail: info@modernizeregistration.org
Web site: www.modernizeregistration.org

Supported by the Rockefeller Family Fund, the Committee to Modernize Voter Registration is a bipartisan group of election administrators, former elected officials, campaign professionals, and experts on voting and elections. The organization aims to inform the discussion regarding voting and elections and to encourage the modernization of our current voter registration system. The organization is committed to providing every eligible American the opportunity to participate in our political process and it supports better reform of the voter registration system.

Democratic Leadership Council (DLC)

600 Pennsylvania Ave. SE, Suite 400, Washington, DC   20003
(202) 546-0007 • fax: (202) 544-5002
e-mail: dlc_admin@dlc.org
Web site: www.dlc.org

The Democratic Leadership Council seeks to promote debate within the Democratic Party and the public at large about national and international policy and political issues. The council opposes electoral districting along party lines and works to modernize voter registration. The organization publishes opinion pieces, policy briefs, and reports on its Web site.

FairVote
6930 Carroll Ave., Suite 610, Takoma Park, MD   20912
(301) 270-4616 • fax: (301) 270-4133
Web site: www.fairvote.org

FairVote acts to transform our elections to achieve universal access to participation, a full spectrum of meaningful ballot choices, and majority rule with fair representation for all. Established in 1992, the organization seeks to build support for innovative strategies to win a constitutionally protected right to vote, universal voter registration, a national popular vote for president, instant runoff voting, and proportional representation. The organization's Web site features research reports, policy briefs, and its periodic *Innovative Analysis* series.

Heritage Foundation
214 Massachusetts Ave. NE, Washington, DC   20002-4999
(202) 546-4400 • fax: (202) 546-8328
e-mail: info@heritage.org
Web site: www.heritage.org

The Heritage Foundation is a conservative public policy organization dedicated to free-market principles, individual liberty, and limited government. Its resident scholars and experts publish position papers and articles on a wide range of issues—such as voter registration, voter fraud, and identification laws—in its numerous publications.

Rock the Vote
1505 22nd St. NW, Washington, DC   20037
(202) 719-9910
Web site: www.rockthevote.com

Rock the Vote's mission is to engage and build the political power of young people to achieve progressive change in the country. Rock the Vote uses music, popular culture, and new technologies to engage and encourage young people to register and vote in every election, providing them the tools to identify, learn about, and take action on the issues that affect their lives and leverage their power in the political process. The organization publishes fact sheets, reports, and news stories on its Web site.

Bibliography

Books

R. Michael Alvarez, Thad E. Hall, and Susan D. Hyde, eds. *Election Fraud: Detecting and Deterring Electoral Manipulation.* Washington, DC: Brookings Institution Press, 2008.

Alec C. Ewald *The Way We Vote: The Local Dimension of American Suffrage.* Nashville, TN: Vanderbilt University Press, 2009.

Paul S. Herrnson, Richard G. Niemi, Michael J. Hanmer, et al. *Voting Technology: The Not-So-Simple Act of Casting a Ballot.* Washington, DC: Brookings Institution Press, 2008.

Marcia Lausen *Design for Democracy: Ballot and Election Design.* Chicago: University of Chicago Press, 2007.

Marc Crispin Miller, ed. *Loser Take All: Election Fraud and the Subversion of Democracy.* Brooklyn, NY: Ig Publishing, 2008.

Francis Fox Piven, Lorraine C. Mennite, and Margaret Groarke *Keeping Down the Black Vote: Race and the Demobilization of American Voters.* New York: New Press, 2009.

William Poundstone *Gaming the Vote: Why Elections Aren't Fair (And What We Can Do About It).* New York: Hill and Wang, 2008.

Aviel David Rubin	*Brave New Ballot: The Battle to Safeguard Democracy in the Age of Electronic Voting.* New York: Morgan Road Books, 2006.
Roy G. Saltman	*The History and Politics of Voting Technology: In Quest of Integrity and Public Confidence.* New York: Palgrave Macmillan, 2006.

Periodicals

Ben Arnoldy	"Are Voter Fraud Fears Overblown?" *Christian Science Monitor*, October 20, 2008.
Edward Blum	"Gerrymandering on Trial," *American Spectator*, March 16, 2009.
eWeek	"What the U.S. Is Doing Wrong with E-Voting," July 30, 2007.
John Fund	"This Will Make Voter Fraud Easier," *Wall Street Journal*, November 2, 2007.
Richard L. Hasen	"Fraud Reform?" *Slate*, February 22, 2006.
John Nienstedt	"Examining the Vote-by-Mail Explosion," *San Diego Union Tribune*, October 27, 2006.
Project Vote	"Voter Fraud Myth Persists, Despite Facts," *AlterNet*, March 14, 2008.
Jim Redden	"Oregon Blazes Mail Trail," *Portland Tribune*, May 16, 2006.

Abigail   "Gerrymandering Democratic Votes,"
Thernstrom   *Forbes*, October 23, 2008.

Time   "Can Voting Machines Work?"
                 October 29, 2006.

Amanda Turkel   "The Fraud of Voter ID Laws,"
                 American Prospect, January 11, 2008.

Ian Urbina   "ID Laws Are Set to Face a Crucial
                 Test," *New York Times*, January 7,
                 2008.

Washington Times "What Is ACORN?" October 10,
                 2008.

Index